REVIVAL ADDRESSES

REVIVAL ADDRESSES

BY

R. A. TORREY

JAMES CLARKE & CO. LIMITED
CAMBRIDGE

First published 1903
Reprinted 1974
S B N 227 67808 7

Published by James Clarke & Co. Ltd,
7 All Saints Passage, Cambridge, U. K.
and distributed by Trade Counter Ltd,
11–14 Stanhope Mews West,
London SW 7 5 RD

Printed in Great Britain
at the University Printing House, Cambridge
(Brooke Crutchley, University Printer)

INTRODUCTION

REQUESTS have come from many quarters for the publication of some of the sermons which God has been pleased to so greatly use in Japan, China, Australia, Tasmania, New Zealand, India, England, and Scotland. This volume is published in response to this request. The author hopes that the sermons may be used as greatly in their printed form as they have been when spoken. The sermons when delivered, as here published, were taken down in shorthand, but have been carefully revised by the author. Each one of them has many sacred memories connected with it. When one of these sermons was delivered through an interpreter in a Japanese city, eighty-seven Japanese came forward and declared publicly their acceptance of Christ. After the delivery of another in Shanghai, a large number of Chinese men and women walked out from their places among their heathen companions and publicly professed their acceptance of Christ. On some occasions in Australia, Tasmania, and New

Zealand, hundreds of men and women came forward and with their own lips publicly confessed their acceptance of Christ as their Saviour and their Lord. Reports of some of these sermons have been given in religious and secular papers, but these reports have been necessarily fragmentary and inaccurate, as they have never been revised by the author. I have abundant proof that even these unsatisfactory reports have done good, but it seems desirable that a full and accurate report of what I have said be given to the public.

CONTENTS

REVIVAL ADDRESSES

I

GOD

"The fool hath said in his heart, There is no God."—Psalm xiv. 1.

I HAVE taken, or rather God has given me, for my text to-night a very short one. I do not think you ever heard a sermon from a shorter text. I will not tell you where to find the text. It occurs several hundred times in the Bible. Indeed, open your Bible at random almost anywhere and you will find my text somewhere on the page. It consists of but one word; but it would take all eternity to exhaust its meaning, and then it will not be exhausted. It is "God"—a word the height and depth and length and breadth of whose meaning no philosopher has ever fully apprehended.

I. God Is

The first thing the Bible teaches us about God is that *God is*. "God is"—two short words. Tremendous significance! "God is." If that simple truth gets hold of your mind and heart it will move and

5

mould your entire life.   It will determine your
science, it will determine your philosophy, it will
determine your daily life, it will determine your
eternity.   " God is."   The psalmist tells us in Psalm
xiv.—" The fool hath said in his heart, There is no
God."   Please note where he says it—" in his heart."
That is, he says there is no God simply because he
does not wish to believe that there is a God.   Now,
there is a God, and a man that denies a fact simply
because he does not wish to believe it is a fool.

There is abundant proof of the existence of God,
so abundant that no man can sit down and consider
the proof thoroughly and candidly without acknow-
ledging the existence of God.   Nature proves the
existence of God.   All through Nature there are
marks of creative intelligence.   Everywhere in Nature you find order, symmetry, law.   You can study
Nature in the minute, or you can study Nature in
the vast, it makes no difference ; everywhere you
find the marks of intelligence and creative design.
You may take your microscope and turn it down
upon the minutest forms of life ; everywhere there
is adaptation to end, to purpose, to design.   The
man of science will tell you that in the minutest
structure discernible by the most powerful microscope he finds perfect beauty, and most perfect
adaptation of means to end.   Or take your tele-
scope and turn it towards the vaster Nature.   Everywhere you see order, symmetry, law, intelligence,
design, all proving an intelligent Creator of the
material universe in which we live.   Suppose I show
you my watch, and ask, " Do you believe it had a
maker ? " you would say, " Certainly."   " But why ?

Did you see it made?" "No." "Did you ever see
a watch made?" "No." "Why, then, do you believe
it had a maker?" "Because everything about it in-
dicates an intelligent maker—hands, figures upon the
face, case, winding apparatus, everything about the
watch proclaims that it had an intelligent maker.
Suppose I replied, "You are mistaken; the watch
had no intelligent maker; the watch came to be
by accident; by a fortuitous concurrence of atoms
dancing around through endless ages, until at last,
in the age in which you find it, they danced into
the present form; thus the watch came to be."
Your remark would be, "That man may think he is
highly educated, but he talks like a fool;" and you
would be right. Yet there are no such marks of
intelligent design in that watch as in this material
universe. One very small part of Nature, your own
eye, is a far more wonderful structure than any watch.
But if some man should stand up and say that this
wonderful universe in which we live came into being
by a fortuitous concurrence of atoms which danced
around through the endless ages until they danced
into their present form, many would call him a
philosopher. In the ordinary affairs of life he would
be called a foolosopher.

But, some one may say, "The doctrine of evolution does away with the whole force of the argument
from design." Not at all. I formerly believed that
the doctrine of evolution was true, but gave up the
belief, not from theological but from scientific reasons,
because it was absolutely unproven; there is not a
single proof of the hypothesis of evolution. People
talk about the missing link; they are all missing;

there is not a single link.   There is not a single place
where one species passes over into another species.
There is not one single observed instance of the
evolution of a higher species from a lower.   Deve-
lopment of varieties there has been, but of evolution of a higher species from a lower not one single
case.   The hypothesis of the evolution of species,
and especially of the highest forms of life from the
lowest, is a guess pure and simple, without one
scientifically observed fact to build upon.   But
suppose the doctrine of evolution were true, it would
not for a moment militate against the argument
from design.   If there were originally some unor-
ganised protoplasm that developed into all the forms
of life and beauty as we see them to-day, it would
be a still more remarkable illustration, in one way,
of the wisdom and power of the Creator, for the
question would arise, Who put into the primordial
protoplasm the power of developing into the universe as we see it to-day ?   It would take a more
wonderful man to make a watch-hand which would
develop into a watch than it would to make a watch
outright.   And, in one way, it would be a more
marvellous illustration of the creative wisdom and
power of God, if God had created some primordial
protoplasm that developed into the world we now
see than if God had made the world at once
as we now see it.   Nature proves that there is
a God.

History proves that there is a God.   You take
one little patch of history, the history of a single
nation or of a few nations, for a few years, and it
sometimes seems like a jangle without meaning, only

portraying the conflicting ambitions and greeds of men. Might, right, and the weakest going to the wall. But take history in a large way, the history of centuries, take all history, and you will see that back of the jarring and conflicting passions, ambitions, combats and struggles of men, there is an all-governing, all-superintending, all-shaping Providence. You see that throughout all history "one increasing purpose runs," "a power, not ourselves, which makes for righteousness." History proves that there is a God.

But there is one special history that proves that there is a God, that is the history of Jesus of Nazaréth as recorded in the gospels of Matthew, Mark, Luke, and John. Great efforts have been put forth to disprove the authenticity of that history; men of the most remarkable genius, of the profoundest scholarship, of untiring activity, have struggled to pull to pieces the history of Jesus Christ as recorded in the four gospels, and every effort of that kind has met with utter failure. The strongest, the ablest, the most remarkable and scholarly effort ever made was that of David Strauss, in the *Leben Jesu*. It seemed to some for awhile, as if David Strauss had succeeded in taking out of the life of Jesus of Nazareth many things commonly believed. But when the life of Jesus Christ by the great German rationalist was itself subjected to criticism, it went to pieces, until there was nothing left. It was utterly discredited. It would not bear careful and candid examination. Renan, with rare subtlety and literary deftness, endeavoured to succeed where Strauss had failed. But his own attempt to eliminate the supernatural from the life of Jesus was less able in almost every way than that of his German predecessor, and failed completely. And every other similar effort to pull to pieces and discredit the life of Jesus Christ, as recorded in the four gospels, has failed absolutely. And to-day it stands established beyond the possibility of candid question that Jesus lived and acted, at least substantially— I believe far more than that—as recorded in the four gospels. It is absolutely impossible for a man to sit down before the four gospels with an unbiassed and honest mind, determined to find out the truth, and come to any other conclusion than that this four gospel record of the life and words and works of Jesus is substantially accurate history.

If Jesus lived as this Gospel says He did, if He wrought as this Gospel says He wrought, healed the sick, cleansed the leper, raised the dead, fed the five thousand with five loaves and two small fishes, and if, above all, having been put to death, He was raised from the dead, it proves to a demonstration that back of the works He performed, back of the resurrection of Jesus Christ, is God. There is a God.

The history of the individual Christian proves the existence of God. I do not depend upon the argument from design or from history—I once did; I do not depend even upon the argument from the life of Jesus Christ—I once did. I know there is a God because I have personal dealings with Him every day of my life. Some subtle philosopher might construct a very specious argument to prove to me that there is no such person as Charles Alexander;

but after all is said I still know that there is, for I have the most intimate relations with him every day of my life. But I have had more intimate dealings with God than with Mr. Charles Alexander. I know that there is a God before I know that there is such a person as Mr. Charles Alexander. I started out years ago on the hypothesis that there was a God, and that God acted as the Bible records that He acts. I determined to put this hypothesis to the most rigid test to see if it worked. I have put that hypothesis to the test during a quarter of a century, and it has never failed. If there had not been a God, or if there had been a God different from the one of whom the Bible tells us, I should have made shipwreck of everything years ago. But the hypothesis has never failed; I have risked my life, reputation, work, everything upon the fact that the God of the Bible is. And, friends, I risked and won. THERE IS A GOD. Therefore the man who says that there is no God is a fool; for any man who denies a fact is a fool. He who denies the supreme fact is a supreme fool. Not only is there a God; but He is the supreme fact of nature, of history, of science, of philosophy, of personal life. Look at the first four words of the Bible, and you will read the profoundest philosophy. "In the beginning, God." In the beginning of nature, God; in the beginning of science, God; in the beginning of human history, God; in the beginning of individual experience, God; in the beginning of everything, God. That is the supreme fact; and he who denies it merely because he does not want to believe it is the supreme fool.

II. GOD IS GREAT

God is great. That thought comes out in the
Bible, from the first verse to the last. Oh, the
majesty of God, the infinite greatness of God! This
whole universe, about which we are learning such
wonderful things every day, is His creative work.
The supreme difference between the teaching of the
Bible and the teaching of modern thought is this—
the teaching of the Bible is an infinite God and an
infinitesimal man, except as God's goodness makes
him great. The teaching of modern literature and
modern thought is—an infinite man and an infinitesimal god. We live in a day that has a very great
man and a very small god. Stop and think. There
are one billion four hundred million people like you
on this earth to-day. You are just one out of that
vast number. Not very big—are you? But wait.
Take the whole earth on which these one billion
four hundred millions live; it is a very small part
of the universe. If the sun were hollow and a hole
bored into it, one million four hundred thousand
earths could be poured into the sun, and still leave
room for them to rattle round. But the sun is only
one sun out of many suns. Our whole solar system
is but one out of many. I was reading an article
the other day, on my way from India, in which an
eminent man of science said that there are probably
at least a million suns as large as ours. Wait a
moment! You are only one out of one thousand
four hundred million persons on this earth. Of
earths such as this upon which we live it would

take more than one million four hundred thousand poured into the sun to fill it. Yet the sun is only one out of a million suns. And there may be a million universes such as ours. And God made them all. That God whose name you dared take upon your lips in vain last night; that God whom you dare philosophise about and say how He ought to act. Take one and divide it by fourteen hundred million multiplied by one million four hundred thousand multiplied by one million multiplied by many millions and that is you. Multiply fourteen hundred million by one million four hundred thousand, and that by one million, and that by many millions, and that by infinity, and that is God. And yet you venture to say how God ought to act. If ever a man appears like a consummate idiot, it is when he tries to tell you how God ought to act. God is infinite, and no number of finites will ever equal the infinite, and the Infinite God is of immeasurably more importance than the whole race of infinitesimal men who inhabit this little globe. Yet you venture to say how God ought to act. Thou fool!

III. GOD IS HOLY

God is holy. How the Bible in every page brings that out! How it labours with all its types, sacrifices, ceremonies, explicit teaching, to impress upon men and women that God is holy. Take the supreme expression of it in 1 John i. 5, "God is light, and in Him is no darkness at all." In the Scripture lesson to-night I read a passage from Isaiah in which he

B

gives us a bit of his own biography. He was, perhaps, the best man of his time, but when he got one
glimpse of God in His holiness, when he saw even
the seraphim (the burning ones, glowing in their
own holiness) covering their faces and their feet in
the presence of the infinitely Holy Jehovah, he was
overwhelmed, and cried, "Woe is me, for I am undone, because I am a man of unclean lips, and I
dwell in the midst of a people of unclean lips, for
mine eyes have seen the King, the Lord of Hosts."
Men and women of London, if there should burst
upon this audience to-night a real vision of God
in His holiness, this whole great gathering would
fall on their faces and cry, "Woe is me, for I am
undone." Not one of you could keep your seats.

IV. We Must all Meet God

Last thought. *You and I some day must meet this
holy God.* The prophet Amos cries, "Prepare to
meet thy God" (Amos iv. 12). Every man and
woman here must some day meet God. The rich
man must meet God! The beggar must meet
God! The scholar must meet God! The illite-
rate man must meet God! The nobleman must
meet God! The king must meet God! The emperor must meet God! Every one must meet
God! The supreme question of life, then, is this:
Are you ready to meet God? None of us can tell
how soon it may be that we shall meet God. The
king of Spain, as the bulletins flashed across the
wires to-night, has been very near meeting his God
to-day. Some of us may meet Him within the next

twenty-four hours; more within the year; many more within five years; and within forty years almost every man and woman in this audience will have met God. Are you ready? If not, I implore you to get ready before leaving this hall to-night.

How can we meet God with joy and not with dismay? There is only one ground upon which man may meet God with joy and not with despair. That ground is the atoning blood of Jesus Christ. God is infinitely holy, and the best of us is but a sinner. The only ground upon which a sinner can meet the holy God is on the ground of the shed blood, the blood of Christ. Any one of us, no matter how outcast or vile, can go boldly into the Holy of Holies on the ground of the shed blood, and the best man or woman that ever walked this earth can meet God on no other ground than the shed blood. There is only one adequate preparation for the sinner to meet God, that is the acceptance of Jesus Christ as our personal Saviour, who bore all our sins on the Cross of Calvary, and as our risen Saviour who is able to set us free from the power of sin.

Men and women, are you ready to meet God? If it be the will of God, I am ready to go up into His presence, and meet Him face to face to-night. Do you say, Have you never sinned? Alas, I have. Sinned so deeply as none of you will ever know, thank God. But, thank God still more, when Jesus Christ was nailed to yonder Cross of Calvary, all my sins were settled. I like a sheep had gone astray. I had turned to my own way, but God laid on Him my sin (Isaiah liii. 6), and the sacrifice God provided

I have accepted. I am ready to meet God face to face to-night and look into those eyes of infinite holiness, for all my sins are covered by the atoning blood.

Are you ready to meet God ? Let me sum up. There is a God. God is great. God is holy. You and I must meet Him. There is only one adequate preparation—the acceptance of Christ as our Sin-bearer, our Saviour, Deliverer from the power of sin. Will you accept Christ to-night ?

II

THE GREATEST SENTENCE THAT WAS EVER WRITTEN

"God is love."—1 JOHN iv. 8.

MY subject is the greatest sentence that was ever written. Of course, that sentence is in the Bible. All the greatest sentences are in the one Book. The Bible has a way of putting more in a single sentence than other writers can put in a whole book. Yet there are some who would tell us that the Bible is no more God's Book than other books. Either they have not read the Bible, or they have read it with their eyes closed.

This sentence has in it but three words. Each word is a monosyllable. One word has four letters, one three, and one only two; yet these nine letters, forming three monosyllables, contain so much of truth that the world has been pondering it for eighteen centuries, and has not got to the bottom of it yet. Whole volumes are dedicated to the exposition of this wonderful sentence—thousands of volumes.

1 John iv. 8, " God is love." That is the greatest sentence that was ever written. That sentence is the key-note of the mission that begins to-day. Everything that you will hear in song or in word

for the next four weeks in this mission revolves round that one central truth, " God is love." That sums up the whole contents of the Bible. If I were asked for a sentence to print in letters of gold on the outside of our Bible, a sentence that summed up the whole contents of the Book, it would be this one, " God is Love." That is the subject of the first chapter of Genesis, it is the subject of the last chapter of Revelation, and it is the subject of every chapter that lies in between.

The Bible is simply God's love story, the story of the love of a holy God to a sinful world. That is the most amazing thing in the Bible. People tell us the Bible is full of things that it is impossible to believe. I know of nothing else so impossible to believe as that a holy God should love a sinful world, and should love such individuals as you and me, as the Bible says He does. But impossible as it is to believe, it is true. There is mighty power in that one short sentence, power to break the hardest heart, power to reach individual men and women who are sunk down in sin, and to lift them up until they are fit for a place beside the Lord Jesus Christ upon the Throne.

When Mr. Moody organised the church in Chicago, of which I am pastor, he was so anxious that everybody should always hear this one truth, and was so afraid that some preacher might come and forget to tell it, that he had it put on the gas jets right above the pulpit, so that the first thing you would see when you went in there on an evening was that text shining out in letters of fire.

One stormy night, before the time of the meeting, the door stood ajar. A man partly intoxicated
saw it open, and thought he might go in and get
warm. He did not know what sort of a place it
was, but when he pushed the door open he saw
that text blazing out, " God is love." He pulled
the door to, and walked away muttering to himself.
He said, " God is not love. If God is love, He
would love me. God does not love a wretch like
me." But it kept on burning down into his soul,
" God is love ! God is love ! God is love !" After
a while he retraced his steps, and took a seat in a
corner. When Mr. Moody walked down after the
meeting, he found the man weeping like a child.
" What is the trouble ? " he asked. " What was it
in the sermon that touched you ? "   " I didn't hear
a word of your sermon."   " Well, what is the
trouble ? "   " That text up there."   Mr. Moody sat
down and from his Bible showed him the way of
life, and he was saved.

I hope it will break some of your hearts. I am
not going to tell you what I think of the love of
God. I am going to give you the Bible's plain
statements about it. There are people who start
out with this text as a foundation, and build a
superstructure of speculation that contradicts the
plain teaching of the very Book from which they
have taken their foundation-stone. Now, nothing
can be more illogical than that. One of two things
is certainly true. Either the Bible is true or it is
not true. If the Bible is not true, we have no
proof that God is love, so that all these universalist
schemes, built on the foundation that " God is love,"

crumble away. If the Bible is true, these schemes which contradict its plain teaching are false. You can take whichever horn of the dilemma you please. Whichever you take, the shallow universalism of the present day crumbles away.

What does the Bible tell us as to how God shows His love ?

1. *That God shows His Love by pardoning Sin.* —Isaiah lv. 7 : " Let the wicked forsake his way, and the unrighteous man his thoughts : and let him return unto the Lord, and He will have mercy upon him ; and to our God, for He will abundantly pardon." God tells us plainly in His Word that He is willing to forgive any sinner that lives, no matter how deep down he has gone, if he will only turn from sin and turn to Him; and He will forgive him the very moment he does so. Of course, God cannot forgive a man while he holds on to his sin, and retain His own moral character.

I have a boy. I love that boy, and I would give a great deal to see him now. I believe there is nothing that boy could do but, if he repented and turned from it, I would forgive him. But I could not forgive him if he held on to his evil way. I could continue to love him and seek to save him, but I could not forgive him. And God cannot forgive us, and remain what He is—a holy God— until we are ready to quit our sin. But the moment we are, He will have mercy upon us, and He will abundantly pardon. If the wickedest man or woman in Edinburgh should have come in to-night—and I hope they have—and should here and now turn from sin, the moment they

did so, God would blot out every sin they ever
committed.

I knew a millionaire in New York City who
turned his back on all his business and money-
making to save the perishing. When he was
going down one of the streets one night, a poor
woman came out of an underground den of infamy
and groaned as he passed. My friend stepped up
to her and told her of the love of God. At first
she would not believe, but he persuaded her that
God loved her. He gave her a shelter. She did
not live long—only about two years—but before she
died, Nellie Conroy stood up before a great audience
in the Cooper Institute, and told them how God
had saved her. Tears were streaming down the
faces of all. A little while after she lay dying;
and, as my friend came into the room, she said:
"Uncle Charlie"—he was not her uncle, but she
called him so for the love she bore—"I will soon
see, in a few hours, little Florence, and I will see
Jesus." And Nellie Conroy, the pardoned and
blood-washed sinner, went up to behold the King.
There is not a man or woman in Edinburgh that
God will not save the moment they turn from their
sin.

2. *God shows His Love by taking account of Sin,
and punishing it.*—Hebrews xii. 6 : "For whom the
Lord loveth He chasteneth, and scourgeth every son
whom He receiveth." People think God will allow
sin to go on unchecked, unrebuked, unpunished.
"God is love," and therefore He takes account of
and punishes sin. There are fathers who are so
selfish that they will not punish their children

when it is necessary for their good. It hurts their feelings, as it does to all true fathers ; and they are so selfish that they sacrifice the welfare of the children in order to spare their own feelings. That is not love but consummate selfishness.

One of my children disobeyed me. I said to myself, " That child must be punished." Oh, how I studied to find some way out, but I could not do it. I knew that for the child's highest welfare punishment must be administered, and the child was punished. I suffered a great deal more than the child, but I loved the child enough to sacrifice my feelings for the child's welfare. God suffers when you and I are punished ; but He loves us so much, that when we need to suffer He administers the suffering Himself.

A gentleman with whom I was staying said to me one day, " Would you like to take a drive ? " We went out to a cemetery, and came to a place where there were three graves. One was long ; it was an adult one, and in it his wife was buried. In the two short graves were the bodies of his two daughters, all he had except a baby boy. We knelt and prayed by the side of the graves. As we were driving back to town the gentleman said, " I pity the man that God has not chastened." What did he mean ? He meant that he had been a man of the world, an upright man, but not a Christian. One night when he came home his wife said, " Porter, one of the children is sick." In a few days she was cold and dead ; and, as she lay in the casket, he knelt down and promised God to take Christ as his Lord and Master. But he lied to God, and forgot all about his resolution. Some time after he came home again, and his wife said, "Porter, the other child is sick." In a few days she also lay cold and dead. Once more he knelt down and promised God that he would become a Christian, *and kept his word*. All the holiest, deepest, purest joys of life had come from his great sorrow.

Are you in sorrow? It is because God loves you. Are there some here resisting the entreaties of God's mercy and grace? I beseech you to repent. I tremble for some men and women, for those who know the way of life, with whom God is striving by His holy Spirit, but who will not come to Him. I tremble for them, because I know that God loves them. You think that is a very strange reason for trembling for a man. No, I know God loves you, and so loves you that, if He cannot bring you in any other way, He will bring you by sorrow and heart-ache.

A friend of mine in Chicago, Colonel Clark, spent his fortune in saving the lost. He went down every night to preach the Gospel in a mission. There was one man who had been attending and resisting God's entreaties of mercy for a long time; and one night as he came along Colonel Clark said, "George, if you do not turn from sin pretty quick, I believe God will take away your wife and child from you, and will lock you up." The man was very angry, and said, "Colonel Clark, you mind your own business; I will mind mine." One month from that night George woke up on the floor of Rochester Jail. His wife was dead, his child had

been taken away from him to be put into better
hands than his. Right there he took Christ as his
Saviour, and now he is a preacher of the Gospel.
Remember, God loves you, and "whom the Lord
loveth He chasteneth."

3. *God shows His Love for us by sympathising
with us.*—Isaiah lxiii. 9: "In all their affliction
He was afflicted." That is one of the wonderful
sentences of this Book. The prophet is speaking
about the children of Israel. Their afflictions were
appalling, and the direct consequence of their own
sin, a judgment sent by the hand of God, and yet
the prophet said God suffered with them in their
sorrow. It is true. There is not a man or woman
here who is in trouble but God sympathises with
you. It may have come in any way, but if you have
any trouble God sympathises with you in it.

Some of you know what it is to have a child
sick for a long time. At first friends came and
sympathised with you, but their sympathy has
grown cold; and, as you have watched day and
night by that fading life, you have said: "There
is no one who sympathises with me." Yes, there is.
God sympathises with you. There are men and
women who have a sorrow of such a character
that they cannot confide it to any human ear;
and they say: "Nobody knows it. Nobody sympathises with me." Yes, there is One who knows,
and He sympathises with you—God.

4. *God shows His Love by His Gifts.*—I cannot
dwell upon that. I just want to speak of one gift.
1 John iii. 1, 2: "Behold, what manner of love
the Father hath bestowed upon us, that we should

be called the sons of God." Oh, that wondrous
gift that God bestowed upon you and me, that
men and women like us should be called children
of God! Oh, what love! Suppose on his coronation day King Edward, after all the ceremonies
were over, had taken his carriage of state, and
had ridden down to the East End of London,
and had seen some ragged, wretched, profane boy,
utterly uneducated and morally corrupt. Suppose
his great heart of love had gone out to that boy,
and, stepping up to that poor wanderer, he had
said: "I love you. I am going to take you in
my carriage to the palace. I am going to dress
you fit to be a king's son, and you shall be known
as the son of King Edward the Seventh." Would
it not have been wonderful? But it would not
have been so wonderful as that the infinitely holy
God should have looked down upon you and me
in our filthiness and rags and depravity, and that
He should have so loved us that He should have
bestowed upon us to be called the sons of God.

5. *God shows His Love by the Sacrifice He has
made for us.*—Sacrifice; after all that is the great
test of love. People tell you that they love you,
but you cannot tell whether they really love you
till the opportunity comes for them to make a
sacrifice for you. I had a friend in the university. We thought a good deal of each other; but
I did not know how much he loved me. Years
after, one night when I was away preaching, this
friend turned up at my house and got to talking
with my wife. He asked a good many leading
questions, and finally got out of her that I was in a

position in which I needed fifteen hundred dollars. He did not say any more at the time, but next day he came to me and said: "You think of doing so and so." "Yes." "That costs money." "I have a scheme to get it." "What is it?" "I have plans." "Well, what are they?" I did not think it was his business, but finally I told him. He said: "It will not work at all. See here. Just let me give you that fifteen hundred dollars." "Well," I said, "I am not going to let any man give me fifteen hundred dollars." "Oh, you can pay it back." "I don't know about that." "I will take my chances." He insisted, and would not take "No" for an answer; he gave me that fifteen hundred dollars, and I have paid it back, but he did not know I would. I knew then that man loved me. God has proved His love. "God so loved the world that He gave"—gave what?— "His only begotten Son"—the best He had, the object of His eternal love—gave Him to suffer and die upon the cruel cross for you and me.

God looked down upon this lost world, upon you and me. He saw that there was only one price that could save us; and He did not stop at that sacrifice. He "so loved the world that He gave His only-begotten Son, that whosoever believeth in Him should not perish, but have everlasting life." That is the most amazing thing in the Bible. You and I sometimes dwell upon the love of Christ, to give up Heaven for us. We look at Him in the courtyard of Pilate, fastened to the whipping-post, with His bare back exposed to the lash of the Roman soldier. We look at Him as the lash cuts into His back again and again, and again, till it is all torn and bleeding. Oh, how He loved us! But looking down from yon throne in heaven was God; and every lash that cut the back of Christ cut the heart of God. We see the soldiers with the crown of thorns, pressing it on His brow, and we see the blood flowing down. Oh, how He loved us! But every thorn that pierced His brow pierced also the heart of God.

Through the dusk of that awful day we see Him on the cross. We hear the last cry, "My God, My God, why hast Thou forsaken Me?" We see how He loved us. But yonder, looking down from the throne of light and glory, was God; and every nail that pierced His hands and feet pierced the heart of God, because He loved you, and you, and you, every one of you. "God so loved the world that He gave His only-begotten Son." Oh, it was wonderful! What are you going to do about this love?

I once heard a story which brought me such a glimpse of God's love as I never had before. I do not know whether it is true or not. A man was set to watch a railway drawbridge over a river. He threw it open and let vessels through. He heard the whistle of a train up the track, and sprang to the lever to bring the bridge back into place, and as he was doing so he accidentally pushed his boy into the river. He heard the cry, "Father, save me; I am drowning." What should he do? The man stood at the post of duty, brought the bridge back so that the train could pass over in safety. Then he jumped into the river to save his boy, but it was too late. He sacrificed his boy to do his duty. When I heard that story I wondered, if it had been my boy, what I would have done. That man owed it to those on the train to do what he did. God owed you and me nothing. We were guilty rebels against Him, but " God so loved the world that He gave His only-begotten Son, that whosoever believeth in Him should not perish, but have everlasting life."

What are you going to do with His love ? Accept it, or trample it under foot ? Accept Christ, and you accept that love: reject Christ, and you trample that love under foot ? I cannot understand how any man or woman in their right senses can harden their hearts against the love of God.

I remember one night at the close of our service we had an after - meeting. The choir were still sitting, and the leading soprano was unconverted — a thoroughly worldly girl. Her mother rose in the meeting, and said, " I wish you would pray for my daughter." I did not look round, but I knew intuitively how that girl looked at that moment. I made it my business to meet her as she was passing out, and said, " Good evening, Cora." Her eyes flashed and cheeks burned ; she was very angry. She said, " My mother ought to have known better. She knows it will only make me worse." I said, " Sit down "; and I turned to Isaiah liii. 5 : " He was wounded for our trans-gressions, He was bruised for our iniquities: the chastisement of our peace was upon Him ; and with His stripes we are healed." I did not say another word. It was not necessary. The anger faded out of those eyes, and burning tears of peni-tence ran down her cheeks. I went from home next

day, and when I came back some one said, "Cora is
sick." I found her very sick, but rejoicing in Jesus.
A few days after her brother came and said,
"We think Cora is dying." I went at once, and
looked on the whitest face I ever saw. She had
not opened her eyes all the morning; but, after I
had finished praying, there came from those lips—
still without opening her eyes—the most wonderful
prayer I ever heard. She thanked God for giving
His Son to die for her. She told Him how she
longed to live to sing to His glory, as she had sung
in the past for herself; but "if it be not Thy will
that I live and sing for Christ, I shall be glad to
depart and to be with Christ." And depart she
did, with a heart conquered, transformed, by the
love of God. What are you going to do with the
love of God?

I have here a story cut from a paper to-day.
Mrs. Bottome, of New York City, says that she had
a friend in her girlhood of whom she lost sight completely for eighteen years. Going back to New York
she was passing along a street, and up in a second
storey window she saw her friend's face, surrounded
by prematurely grey hair. She ran up to the door
of the house, and said to the maid, "Take that card
to your mistress." "She is not at home," was the
answer. "Oh yes, she is: I saw her at the window";
and Mrs. Bottome rushed past the maid up into the
room, and they fell into one another's arms. "What
has become of you for all these years?" asked Mrs.
Bottome. The answer was, "Come into the other
room, and I will show you." In a room magnificently
fitted up there sat an idiot boy of seventeen years of

c

age, scarcely able to talk—a drivelling idiot. His mother said, " My duty lies here, with my darling boy." Mrs. Bottome says that in a moment of thoughtlessness she asked, " How can you endure it ? I do not wonder you are prematurely grey." " I knew you would not understand my love for my sweet boy," said her indignant friend. " It is no burden, no care, to live and serve my boy ; and if, some day, he will only give one sign that he recognises me as his mother, I will feel repaid for all the years of love I have lavished on him."

That was but a faint image of the love of God. What are you going to do with this love of God ? That boy did not repay his mother's love ; for, as Mrs. Bottome says, he was an idiot and did not know any better. You are not idiots. You know God's love : how are you going to repay it ?

III

"FOUND WANTING"

"Tekel ; Thou art weighed in the balances, and art found wanting."—Daniel v. 25.

Any one who loves the drama should read the Bible, for the Bible is the most dramatic book that was ever written. There is nothing to compare with it in Æschylus or Sophocles or Euripides among the ancients, or in Shakespeare among the moderns, in striking situations, in graphic delineation, and in startling *dénouement*.

One of the most intensely interesting and at the same time suggestive scenes in the Bible is that described in Daniel v.—Belshazzar's feast. Belshazzar was not the supreme king of Babylon. Nabonidus, his father, was king, and had associated him with himself on the throne ; Belshazzar was second ruler in the kingdom. The critics used to tell us there never was such a king as Belshazzar ; but Sir William Rawlinson dug up a tablet from Nabonidus himself, on which he speaks of his son Belsharuzzar ; and again the critics, as so often before, were brought to grief by the discoveries of modern archæology.

But now Belshazzar was in supreme command in the city. His father Nabonidus had been shut outside the city walls by the forces of Cyrus. Puffed up by the pride of his newly-gotten power, Belshazzar makes a great banquet. The palace is a blaze of light. The long tables are set for more than a thousand guests. They are brilliant and dazzling with plates and cups and tankards of silver and gold, many-jewelled, reflecting back the light from countless candelabra. Reclining at the tables are the guests, with fingers and arms ringed and jewelled. The air is heavy with perfume and tremulous with the music of harp and dulcimer and sackbut. Between the tables the oriental women weave through the contortions and distortions of the Asiatic dance. Back and forth across the table fly jest and repartee.

In the midst of this hilarity a strange and daring conceit enters the mind of the royal entertainer. Belshazzar whispers to his chief steward a secret command. The guests are all agog with curiosity to know what the mysterious mandate may be. Their curiosity is soon gratified; for the chief steward, followed by a host of retainers, comes in bearing in their arms the cups of gold and silver which Nebuchadnezzar had carried away from the temple of Jehovah after the sack of the city of Jerusalem. Belshazzar commands that the cups be filled with Babylonian wine, and passed from lip to lip—while he and his guests sing the praises of the gods of gold and of silver, of brass, of iron, of wood, and of stone.

The hilarity becomes more boisterous. Louder and louder thrum the instruments, faster and faster spin the feet of the dancers, swifter and swifter

fly jest and repartee. Suddenly a hush like death
falls upon the banqueting - hall. One of the
revellers, lifting his eyes to the wall, sees the
fingers of a man's hand writing. As he gazes in
wonder he becomes the centre of observation, and
all eyes turn in the same direction. Now the king
turns and looks also. There, writing in characters
of fire, are the mysterious fingers of an armless
hand. Terror freezes Belshazzar to the very soul.
In the graphic language of the prophet Daniel,
" the king's countenance was changed, and his
thoughts troubled him, so that the joints of his
loins were loosed, and his knees smote one against
another." In a few moments Belshazzar pulls himself together, and hoarsely cries, " Bring hither the
astrologers, the Chaldeans, and the soothsayers."

In come the magi of Babylon, splendidly ap-
parelled, with proud and stately tread. Expecta-
tion rises high in their hearts. They think that
by their cunning arts they can deceive the king,
and gain new emoluments; but only for a moment.
The look of confidence fades from their faces. The
writing is beyond their art.

Again terror lays hold on Belshazzar. Again his
countenance was changed in him. The queen-
mother hears the confusion. She walks in with
stately tread, and tries to reassure her royal son.
" O king, live for ever: let not thy thoughts trouble
thee, nor let thy countenance be changed: there is
a man in thy kingdom, in whom is the spirit of the
holy gods." And she proceeds to sing the praises
of Daniel. " Let Daniel be called, and he will show
the interpretation." Daniel is summoned. Bel-

shazzar turns to him, and says, " O Daniel, I have heard of thee, that the spirit of the gods is in thee, and that light and understanding and excellent wisdom is found in thee. And I have heard of thee, that thou canst make interpretations, and dissolve doubts : now if thou canst read the writing, and make known to me the interpretation thereof, thou shalt be clothed with scarlet, and have a chain of gold about thy neck, and shalt be the third ruler in the kingdom."

Daniel, with noble pride, scorns the proffered gifts. " Let thy gifts be to thyself, and give thy rewards to another. I will have none of them ; but I will read yonder writing, and make known to thee the interpretation." But first Daniel proceeds to rebuke the blasphemous daring of Belshazzar. He recalls the history of Nebuchadnezzar, his grand-father, and how God had humbled his stout-hearted pride. Then he says, " The God in whose hand thy breath is, and whose are all thy ways, hast thou not glorified though thou knewest all this : then was the part of the hand sent from Him ; and this writing was written. And this is the writing that was written, MENE, MENE, TEKEL, UPHARSIN. This is the interpretation of the thing :

" MENE ; God hath numbered thy kingdom, and finished it.

" TEKEL ; Thou art weighed in the balances, and art found wanting.

" PERES ; Thy kingdom is divided, and given to the Medes and Persians."

Belshazzar calls for the royal robe, and it is placed on Daniel. A chain of gold is cast about his neck, and he is proclaimed next to Belshazzar, third ruler in the kingdom. The royal banquet goes on. The hilarity increases; but, hark! the tramp, tramp, tramp, tramp of soldiers' feet in the streets of Babylon. The armies of Cyrus have turned the waters of the Euphrates, and have come in by the river-bed and the two-leaved gates of Babylon.

There is a crashing sound at the gate. The guests look round for a place to flee. But it is too late. Tramp, tramp, tramp, up the palace stairs, with a crash and a rush, the Persian and Median soldiers come in. Swords flash in air for a moment. Belshazzar looks up, and sees the sword over his head. It falls. Belshazzar is a corpse. " That night was Belshazzar the king of the Chaldeans slain." I call your attention to one word on the wall:

" TEKEL; Thou art weighed in the balances, and art found wanting."

In whose balances was Belshazzar weighed? The balances of God. Not in the balances of his own estimation of himself: he would never have been found wanting there. Not in the balances of public opinion: the men of Babylon would have said, " Belshazzar is the greatest of our statesmen, and the coming man." Not in the balances of human philosophy. In the balances of God.

Every man and woman here to-night is to be weighed in the same balances, the balances of God. How much do you suppose that you weigh in the balances of God? I do not ask you how much you weigh in your own opinion of yourself. That is of no consequence, for many a man who thinks most

of himself is of least account in the mind of God.
I do not ask how much you weigh in the balances
of public opinion. You may be a leading citizen
and a chief magistrate, whom all delight to honour ;
but oftentimes that which is highly esteemed among
men is abomination in the sight of God.

How much do you think you weigh in the
balances of God ? There are some of us who set
much store by our morality, our culture, and our
refinement ; but if we knew how little we weighed
in the balances of the eternal and all holy God, we
would fall on our knees and cry, " God be merciful
to me a sinner."

Is there any way in which we can tell how much
we weigh in the balances of God ? There is.
God has given to us the weights wherewith He
weighs us.

Turn to Exodus xx. and you will get the first
ten weights by which God weighs men—the well-
known Ten Commandments. Let me read them.

" Thou shalt have no other gods before me."
What is a man's god ? A man's god is the thing
he thinks most of. If a man thinks more of money
than anything else, money is his god ; and many a
citizen of Edinburgh worships Plutus, the god of
wealth. Many a man is sacrificing conscience,
sacrificing honour, sacrificing obedience to God, to
gain money. You do things in business that you
know are not according to the teachings of the
Bible, things that you know are not pleasing to
a holy God, because there is money in them. Gold
is your god, and you are found wanting by the
first of God's commandments. There are men who

worship gold just as really as if they had a
sovereign hung up in their bedchamber, and said
their prayers to it.

Many worship social position. How many are
doing things in matters of dress and in matters of
social life that are disapproved by conscience! But
it is what society does; and they think that if they
do not do the same they will lose their position in
society. You are putting society before God.
Society is your god. You are weighed and found
wanting by the first of God's laws.

Major Whittle once went, in Washington, to call
upon a man who had been prominent in public and
church life. He was showing Major Whittle over
his beautiful new house. They came to a large
and beautiful room, and Major Whittle asked,
"What is this for?" The man was silent at first.
"What is this for?" asked Major Whittle again.
The man hung his head, and said, "Well, Major, if
you must know, this is a ball-room." "What! a
ball-room. Do you mean to tell me that you have
sunk so low that you have a ball-room in your
house?" "Well, Major, I never thought I would
come to this; but my wife and daughter said we
were in society now, that this was the thing in
Washington, and that we must have it to keep our
position in Washington society." Social position
was their god; and that man paid for it dearly in
the wreck and ruin of his home.

Many a man worships whisky. How many a man
is sacrificing his brain-power, his business capacity,
the respect of his fellow-citizens, the reverence of
his wife and children, in devotion to the cursed

whisky. I saw many a hideous god when I was travelling in India, all sorts of beastly images which men bow down before and worship, but I know no god more beastly, no god more disgusting than this god of whisky, upon the altar of which men are offering as a sacrifice their children and their interests.

How many a young man and young woman worships the god of pleasure. They are doing things for pleasure that their conscience disapproves of, things that hinder communion with God. They are sacrificing everything that they may have amusement and pleasure. Amusement is their god. Weighed and found wanting by the first weight of the ten commandments.

I have no time to dwell upon the second command: "Thou shalt not make unto thee any graven image, or any likeness of any thing that is in heaven above, or that is in the earth beneath, or that is in the water under the earth: thou shalt not bow down thyself to them, or serve them, for I the Lord thy God am a jealous God, visiting the iniquity of the fathers upon the children unto the third and fourth generation of them that hate Me, and showing mercy unto thousands of them that love Me, and keep My commandments."

The Third Command: "Thou shalt not take the name of the Lord thy God in vain ; for the Lord will not hold him guiltless that taketh His name in vain."—How much do you weigh when you are weighed by that law ! Oh how many a man on your streets breaks that law ! And men not only break it, but they think it a light matter. They think that law is of no consequence. When you approach men and speak to them about Christ, they will say, " Well, but I do not know that I need Christ. I am not a very bad man. I have never stolen anything. I have never killed anybody. I have never committed adultery. Oh, I do swear occasionally." They think it a light matter, but God does not regard it so. " Thou shalt not take the name of the Lord thy God in vain; for the Lord will not hold him guiltless that taketh His name in vain."

If there is any sin which shows that the very foundations of a man's character are honey-combed and rotten, it is the sin of profanity. You cannot trust a profane swearer anywhere. A profane swearer is ripe for any crime. What is the only foundation for a sound character ? Reverence for God; and when that is gone the foundation of character is gone. Character may not crumble away at once, as a building does not always fall the moment its foundation is rotten, in a measure, but it will fall. The foundation is gone. No man can swear profanely until he has gotten very, very low in the moral scale. A man has to go down pretty low (has he not ?) to speak disrespectfully of his mother. We have seen men go pretty far into sin, and yet have so much manhood left that, when others spoke insultingly about their mother, they would resent it. A man has fallen very low who will speak lightly of his mother; but a man has got immeasurably lower before he will speak profanely of God. The purest mother is nothing to the all holy One. No mother ever loved a child, no mother ever sacrificed for a child, as God has loved you and made sacrifices for you; and if you can take God's name upon your lips in profanity you are a vile wretch. I beseech of you get on your face before the eternal God before you sleep, and cry to Him for mercy.

But there are other ways of taking God's name in vain besides profane swearing. Much that we call praying is taking God's name in vain. Every time you have knelt down to pray and have had no thought of God in your heart while you take His name upon your lips, you have taken God's name in vain. In the Church of England you go through those marvellously beautiful prayers in the ritual, but when you do it as a mere matter of form, with no thought of God in your mind, you have taken God's name in vain. You repeat that wonderful prayer that the Master himself taught us: " Our Father which art in heaven, hallowed be Thy name. Thy kingdom come. Thy will be done in earth as it is done in heaven. Give us this day our daily bread; and forgive us our trespasses as we forgive those that trespass against us. And lead us not into temptation, but deliver us from evil. For thine is the kingdom, and the power, and the glory, for ever and ever." All the time you recite it you have not one thought what you are saying. It is downright appalling profanity.

The Fourth Command : " Remember the Sabbath day, to keep it holy. Six days shalt thou labour, and do all thy work, but the seventh day "—not the seventh day of the week, as some men say, daring to put into God's Word what He did not put in, but the

seventh day for rest after six days of work, without
specifying which day of the week it should come.
Of course it was the seventh day of the week with
the Jew, in commemoration of the old creation; but
with the Christian it is the first day of the week, in
commemoration of the new creation through a Risen
Lord. "The seventh day is the Sabbath of the Lord
thy God; in it thou shalt not do any work, thou,
nor thy son, nor thy daughter, thy manservant,
nor thy maidservant, nor thy cattle, nor thy
stranger that is within thy gates: for in six days
the Lord made heaven and earth, the sea, and
all that in them is, and rested the seventh day:
wherefore the Lord blessed the Sabbath day, and
hallowed it." There was a day when Scotchmen
kept that law. It may be you do now; but, alas,
in India I saw a thing that stirred my blood and
sickened my heart. I saw Scotchmen—not merely
Englishmen and Irishmen—I saw Scotchmen, from
the land of the Covenanters, on God's holy day, not
in the house of God, but off playing golf, riding on
their wheels, engaging in all manner of amusement.
I do not know whether you do it at home or not;
but the land, the city, the individual who forgets the
Sabbath day has undermined the foundations of
God's favour and its own prosperity.

The Fifth Command: "Honour thy father and
thy mother: that thy days may be long upon the
land which the Lord thy God giveth thee."—
I wish I had time to dwell upon that; for we are
getting into a day when the young think they know
more than their parents, speaking lightly about
"the old man" and "the old woman." They think

father and mother are old fogies, and that the young people know it all. They disobey their parents. The child who disobeys a parent will bring upon his own head the curse of God. There is only one law superior to the law of father and mother; and that is the law of God. Even those who are grown up, and do not treat the father and mother with the respect and consideration which they should, will reap what they sow. God have mercy upon the one, young or old, who breaks that commandment.

The Sixth Command: "Thou shalt not kill."— How much do you weigh by that law? You say, "I am all right by that law. We have no murderers here." Are you absolutely sure? "Why, certainly. Where do you think you are talking? Down in the Grassmarket?" No, I am talking in the Synod Hall; but there are other ways of killing people besides driving a dagger into their heart or firing a bullet into their brain. A husband can kill his wife by neglect, and cruelty, and unfaithfulness. How many a woman is hastening to an early grave, with a broken heart, because she has learned that the man who swore to be true to her is unfaithful.

One day I was talking with a very brilliant man, who was under the influence of liquor. I said to him, "John, you ought to take Jesus Christ." "Oh," was his reply, "you know I do not believe as you do. I am one of these new theologians. I have a broader theology than you have. I am one of those believers in the eternal hope. You do not believe that old-fashioned theology, do you? Now, honestly, suppose I should drop right down here now, what

would become of me ? " I said, " John, you would go
straight to hell, and you would deserve to go."
" What have I done ? " " I will tell you. You have
got your wife's heart under your heel, and you are
grinding the life out of it. What is worse, you are
trampling under foot the Christ of God, who died
on the Cross of Calvary to save you."

How many a son is killing his mother by his
wild dissolute life. I remember staying in a beautiful home, where there was everything that wealth
could buy. One would have thought that the
mistress of that home must be a perfectly happy
woman. But she would rise in the middle of the
night, and walk up and down the halls of her
beautiful home with a breaking heart. A few
months after she died. Why ? She had a wandering boy. She did not even know where he was ;
and as I stood by her grave, with that wandering
boy, who had come to her dying bed, I thought in
my heart, " Murdered by her wayward son."

Some of you are hastening your mother's foot-
steps to the grave. You have not written your
mother for six months. In Melbourne a man came
rushing down the hall and said, " Oh, I have killed
my mother." He rushed into the inquiry room,
and was led to Christ. Is there a man here who
is killing his mother ? Repent, take Christ ; write
to your mother to-night that you are saved.

There are other ways of murdering people. I do
not know whether it is common in Scotland. I
think, and I certainly hope, not. But it is common
where Scotchmen have gone. How shall I describe
it ? The most appalling kind of murder in the

world. Mothers murdering their own helpless babes, to escape the responsibility of what is one of the greatest privileges in the world, a large family. If there is any hand in the world that is scarlet with the blood of murder, it is that of the woman who murders her own unborn babe ; and there are men who call themselves physicians who will act as helpers in this hellish business. Such a one ought not to put " M.D " after his name, but " D.M."—damnable murderer. In our country they hang them, which is just. Alas, they do not always catch them. I said this in an Australian city, and the wife of a physician was very indignant about it. But her indignation did not alter the truth of what I said. It only exposed a guilty party.

The Seventh Command : " Thou shalt not commit adultery."—I cannot dwell on that. It needs to be dwelt upon, but not here. Simply let me say that there is no class of sins upon which God has set the stamp of His disapproval in a plainer way, by the fearful consequences that immediately follow the sins covered by this commandment. The woman untrue to her husband, the husband untrue to his wife : the curse of God always follows them. It may be done by legal means, under the cover of divorce laws that controvert God's laws, but it does not lessen the sin. The meanest scoundrel that walks the earth, the meanest man alive, is the man who steps in, under any circumstances, between a man and his wife ; and the meanest woman on earth is the one who steps in between another woman and her husband. Remember, furthermore, that our Saviour interpreted this law as applying not only to the overt act, but to the secret thought of the heart, when He said, " Whoso looketh on a woman to lust after her hath committed adultery with her already in his heart."

The Eighth Command : "Thou shalt not steal."— How much do you weigh, weighed by that law? Wait a moment. What is it to steal? To steal is to take property from another without giving an adequate equivalent in either property or money. For example, every man who sells goods under false pretences is a thief. The man who sells a piece of cloth as being "all wool" when it is part cotton, is a thief. The man who employs labour, and takes advantage of the poor man's necessity, and does not give him in pay a full equivalent for his labour, is a thief. Every labouring man who does not give to his employer, in good honest work, a fair equivalent for the wages paid to him, is a thief. The gambler who gambles and wins is a thief. Every time you bet on cards, on a horse race, on a boat race, every time you invest in pools or in a lottery, whether it be a public lottery or a church lottery, and win, you are a thief. The man who gambles and wins is a thief: the man who gambles and loses is a fool. So every gambler is either a thief or a fool.

The Ninth Command : "Thou shalt not bear false witness against thy neighbour."—I know you do not like what I am saying, but that does not alter it; and you will not escape God by trying to forget what I say. But if you do not pay attention to my words, as far as they are true, they will rise up against you in the day of judgment.

How much do you weigh, weighed by that com-

D

mandment? "Well," you say, "I am all right by that,
because I was never in court." Does it say anything
about court?   Every time you tell anything about
another that is derogatory to them, and is not true,
you have broken this law of God. You hear a story,
and do not take pains to find out whether it is true
or not.   Perhaps you add a bit to it, and go on and
tell it, and it is not true. You have broken the law
of God.   You say, "I thought it was true." It is
not what you think: it is the fact.   Whenever you
hear anything against a neighbour, do not believe it
until it is proven absolutely to be true; and even
when it is, keep it to yourself, unless duty clearly
demands the telling of it, which is very seldom.

Some of you say, "Did you hear that awful story
about Mrs. —— ?   I was awfully sorry." You lie.
You were glad to hear it, or you would have kept it
to yourself. The gossip, the slanderer, is viler than
the vilest thief that walks your streets. The thief
only steals money: the slanderer steals what money
cannot buy—reputation.

The Tenth Command: "Thou shalt not covet thy
neighbour's house, thou shalt not covet thy neighbour's wife, nor his manservant, nor his maidservant,
nor his ox, nor his ass, nor anything that is thy
neighbour's."——God's law covers not only the overt
act, but the covert thought of the heart as well.
Many of you would not steal your neighbour's
horse, but you wish it was yours. You would not
run off with your neighbour's wife, but you wish
she were yours. You would not rob your neighbour
of his money, but you wish it was your money.
You have broken the law of God.

How much do you weigh, weighed by the law of God ?

There are two other weights heavier than these. Matthew vii. 12 : "All things whatsoever ye would that men should do to you, do ye even so to them." The so-called Golden Rule. How many talk about it, and how few keep it.

One day I was talking to a sea-captain. I asked him, "Captain, why are you not a Christian ?" "The Golden Rule is a good enough religion for me," he replied. "Do you keep it ?" He dropped his head. He talked about it, but he did not keep it. Talking about it will not save you. Do you do it ? Mind it does not merely put it negatively, "Do not do to others whatsoever ye would not that they should do to you." That is Confucianism. The Christian rule is positive. "Do these things to them." Sell goods to other people just the way you want other people to sell goods to you. Talk about other people behind their backs just as you want them to talk about you behind your back. Do you do it ? Always ? Then you are weighed and found wanting.

The heaviest weight of all is in Matthew xxii. 37, 38 : "Thou shalt love the Lord thy God with all thy heart, and with all thy soul, and with all thy mind. This is the first and great commandment." How much do you weigh by that law ? Put God first in everything—in business, in politics, in social life, in study, in everything. Do you do it ? Have you always done it ? No, you say, I have not. Then you are weighed and found wanting, not only by breaking a law of God, but this is "the first and the great command;" you have broken the first and greatest of God's laws.

A minister asked me to talk to a young man who wanted to go into the ministry. He was a splendid looking fellow. When he came to me, I said, "You want to go into the ministry. Are you a Christian?" "Why, of course I am. I was brought up a Christian, and I am not going back on the training of my parents." "Have you been born again?" "What?" "Jesus says, 'Except a man be born again, he cannot see the kingdom of God.'" "Well," he said, "I have never heard of that before." "Did you know you had committed the greatest sin a man can commit?" "No, I never did." "What do you think it is?" "Murder." "You are greatly mistaken. Let us see what God says." I turned to Matthew xxii. 37, 38, and read: "Thou shalt love the Lord thy God with all thy heart, and with all thy soul, and with all thy mind. This is the first and great commandment." "Which commandment is it?" I asked. "The first and greatest." "Have you kept it? Have you loved God with all your heart, and all your soul, and all your mind? Have you put God first in everything—in business, in pleasure, in social life, in politics?" "No, sir. I have not." "What have you done then?" "I have broken this commandment." "Which commandment is it?" "The first and greatest." "What have you done then?" "I have broken the first and greatest of God's commandments. I have committed the greatest sin a man can commit. But I never saw it before."

How much do we weigh, every one of us, including the preacher ? Every one of us is weighed and found wanting. What shall we do then ? This is where the Gospel comes in. I have preached up to this point nothing but law. God has weighed the whole world in the balances and found it wanting, and in Christ He provided salvation for a wanting world.

God sent His Son, who kept that law, and then died for you and me who have broken it ; and all you and I have to do is to take Christ into the balances with us. Christ can weigh up all the weights. When we take Christ into the balance with us, then we are weighed, and found not wanting.

Will you take Jesus Christ into the balances with you to-night ? Woe to the man who is weighed in the balances of God for the last time without having Jesus Christ with him. This may be the last opportunity for some ; it may at all events be the last opportunity which you will ever take. The time will come when you will be weighed and found wanting ; and you will look back and say, " Oh, why did I not listen to the preacher ? " You will remember this sermon and the text ; and you will say, " Oh, if I only had improved the opportunity ! "

Mr. Moody told a story I shall never forget. A man was set to watch a drawbridge. He had orders not to open the draw until a special train passed. Boat after boat came up and urged him to open the bridge and let them through. " No, I have my orders to wait till the special passes." At last a friend came up and over-urged him, and he allowed

himself to be persuaded. He threw the draw open.
No sooner was the bridge well open and the vessels
beginning to enter, than he heard the whistle of
the special. He sprang to the lever, but he was
too late. The train came on with lightning speed.
He looked on as it dashed into the open chasm,
he heard the shrieks of the injured and saw the
corpses of the dead, and went mad. He never re-
covered his senses, but walked up and down the
padded cell of the asylum, crying, " Oh ! if I only
had ; oh ! if I only had." Had what ? Obeyed
orders. Men and women reject Christ, for the last
time, and you will walk up and down the eternal
madhouse wringing your hands, and saying, " Oh !
if I only had ; oh ! if I only had." Had what ?
Obeyed God, and accepted His Son as your Saviour.
Will you do it now ?

IV

THE JUDGMENT DAY

"God now commandeth all men everywhere to repent; because He hath appointed a day, in the which He will judge the world in righteousness by that man whom He hath ordained; whereof He hath given assurance unto all men, in that He hath raised him from the dead."—ACTS xvii. 30, 31.

THERE are two events in the future which are absolutely certain. First of all, it is absolutely certain that Jesus Christ is coming again to receive His people unto himself, and to reward them according to their works; and in the second place, it is absolutely certain that Jesus Christ is coming again to judge the world. When I was on the ocean some months ago a man asked me one night, as we were walking the deck of the great steamer together, "What will be the outcome of this tendency towards great trusts and monopolies in business?" And I replied, "I do not know." Men often come to me with the question, "What will be the outcome of these great combinations of labouring men to resist the encroachments of capital?" And again I reply, "I don't know."

But I will tell you what I do know, and it is infinitely more important. I know that some day the Lord Jesus Christ will come back again, and receive His waiting and faithful people unto himself;

and I know that there is going to be a judgment
day for the world, and that judgment day is the
subject of our thought to-night.

There are five things about the judgment day
that are set forth in our text : first, the certainty of
it ; secondly, the universality of it; thirdly, the
basis of it ; fourthly, the administrator of it ; and,
lastly, the issues of it.

I. *First, the Certainty of it.*—It is absolutely
certain that there is to be a judgment day. " God
hath appointed a day in which He will judge the
world in righteousness."   Men who are living in
sin may laugh at it; they cannot laugh it away.
In the days of Noah men laughed at Noah's predictions that there was to be a flood, but the flood
came and swept them all away.   In the days of
Lot the men of Sodom laughed at the idea that
God would rain fire and brimstone out of heaven,
and destroy Sodom and Gomorrah and the other
cities of the plain ; but the fire and brimstone fell,
and these cities were blotted out.   In the days of
Jeremiah the people of Jerusalem laughed at
Jeremiah's predictions that Nebuchadnezzar would
come and lay Jerusalem in the dust, and destroy
their temple.   But it all came to pass just as God
said, and just as Jeremiah believed and predicted.
In the days of Jesus Christ men laughed at Christ's
prediction that the armies of Rome under Titus and
Vespasian would lay Jerusalem's walls even with
the ground, and that calamity would overtake that
city such as the world had never seen; but his-
torians outside the Bible tell us that it all came to
pass just as Christ predicted, and that Jerusalem

was overtaken with the most appalling siege in the world's history. All of God's predictions about judgment on individuals and nations in the past have come true to the very letter in spite of all the false hopes that were held out by false prophets.

If we are to judge the future by the past—and there is no other way to judge it—God's predictions about the future with regard to judgment upon individuals and nations will come true to the very letter, in spite of all the false hopes held out by the false prophets; that is, by the "liberal preachers" of the day. It is absolutely certain that there is to be a judgment day for the world.

God has given us a special guarantee of the judgment day, and that special guarantee is the resurrection of Christ from the dead. As we read in the text, "God will judge the world in righteousness by that man whom He hath ordained; *whereof He hath given assurance unto all men, in that He hath raised Him from the dead.*" The resurrection of Jesus Christ from the dead is an absolutely certain fact of history. It is not a theological fiction; it is not a poet's dream : it is an established fact of history. If I had time to-night to go into the evidence, I could prove to every fair-minded, thinking, man that, beyond question, Jesus Christ rose from the dead. When we were in the city of Sydney, I was talking to the business men of Sydney and Members of both Houses of Parliament there for four hours, to prove to them that Christ did rise from the dead, and many an Agnostic, Deist, Unitarian, and Higher Critic had his views utterly shattered, and turned to the risen Christ. There is no time,

however, to-night to go into the evidence of the
resurrection of Jesus Christ. I simply want to say
to you that the evidence for the resurrection of
Jesus Christ is so overwhelming that it is impossible
for any honest man to sit down and thoroughly
sift the evidence, and come to any other conclusion
than that Christ did rise from the dead.

Years ago there were two eminent lawyers, one
named Lyttleton and the other West. These two men
were Deists ; that is, they had faith in a Supreme
Being, but did not believe in revelation, or in
inspiration, or in the miraculous. One day they
got to talking about their views, and finally one
said to the other, " Well, we cannot maintain our
position until we disprove two things ; first, the
reputed conversion of Saul of Tarsus, and secondly,
the reputed resurrection of Jesus Christ from the
dead." Said Lyttleton to West, " I will write a
book to prove that Saul of Tarsus was never
converted in the way which the Acts of the
Apostles record." And said West to Lyttleton,
" I will write a book to prove that Jesus Christ
did not rise from the dead as the evangelists say."
Well, they wrote their books, and when they met
afterwards, West said to Lyttleton, " How have
you got on ? " " I have written my book," said
Lyttleton, " but as I have studied the evidence
from a legal standpoint, I have become convinced
that Saul of Tarsus was converted in just the
way the Acts of the Apostles say he was, and
I have become a Christian. How have you got
on ? "   " Well," said West, " I have sifted the
evidence for the resurrection of Jesus Christ from

the legal standpoint, and I am satisfied that Jesus of Nazareth was raised from the dead just as Matthew, Mark, Luke, and John record, and I have written my book in defence of Christianity." And these two books can be seen in our libraries to-day. It is absolutely impossible for any man with a legal mind, and accustomed to sift evidence, to sit down and thoroughly investigate the evidence for the resurrection of Jesus Christ, and come to any other conclusion than that Jesus of Nazareth rose from the dead. Well, that resurrection of our Lord Jesus Christ is a guarantee that a judgment day is coming. When Jesus Christ came upon the earth He claimed in John v. 22, 23, "The Father judgeth no man, but hath committed all judgment unto the Son; that all men should honour the Son, even as they honour the Father. He that honoureth not the Son honoureth not the Father which hath sent Him." He claimed that there was a judgment day coming and that He was to be the Judge. Men hated him for making the claim, and the other claim involved in it, the claim of Deity. They put Him to death for making this claim, but before they put Him to death He said, "My Father will set his seal to the claim for which you put me to death." And when the third day came, the breath of God swept through the sleeping clay, and God, by the resurrection of Christ, set His seal to Christ's claims, and said in accents that cannot be mistaken and that are a message to all ages, "There is a judgment day coming." The indisputable resurrection of Jesus Christ in the past points with unerring finger to a

certain judgment in the future.   If there is any
man here to-night that flatters himself that there is
to be no judgment day; if there is any man here
that fancies that he can go on in sin and never be
called to account for it; if there is any man here
that believes he can go on trampling under foot the
Son of God, and not have to suffer for it, oh, man,
throw that hope away to-night for it is baseless.
It is absolutely certain that there will be a day
in which Jesus Christ will judge the world in
righteousness.

II. *The Universality of the Judgment.*—In the
second place please note the universality of the
judgment day.   "God hath appointed a day
in which He will judge *the world.*"   It will be no
class judgment; every man and woman on the
face of this earth will have to face the Judge in
that day.   Of course all who are Christians, all
who have accepted Christ as their Saviour, and
surrendered to Him as their Lord, will have been
caught up to meet Him in the air.   But all the
rest will have to face the Judge in that day.   There
will be no escaping that day.   Men often escape
human courts.   There is many a thief that has
never been arrested, there is many a murderer
that remains unhung; but when God sends forth
His officers to gather the people for that judgment day, they will have to come, and they will
have to stay right there until their case is settled.
Men have often escaped me when I am preaching.
When the preaching becomes too pointed, they
get up and go out, and thus they escape me.
You can't escape God that way.   You will have

to come there, and you will have to stay there until your case is decided. He is going to judge the world in righteousness. How you would rejoice if every infidel in London were at this meeting to-night. But most infidels would not dare to come to this meeting. But there will be a meeting that every infidel will be at. There will be one meeting that every hypocritical church member will be at. There will be a meeting where every unpenitent sinner will be present—the meeting with Jesus Christ at the judgment bar of God. That man who is sitting in this meeting to-night trying to make light of every-thing I am saying—you will be at that meeting, and you will not make light of it; you will be there face to face with Jesus Christ. That woman who has come to this meeting to-night for any purpose but a good one, you will meet Christ there at the judgment bar of God.

III. *The Basis of the Judgment.*—In the third place note the basis of judgment.

1. " The deeds done in the body." In 2 Corinthians, chapter v., verse 10, are the words, " For we must all appear before the judgment seat of Christ; that every one may receive the things done in his body according to that he hath done, whether it be good or bad." *The deeds done in the body* are the basis of that judgment. There are preachers who tell us that a man can die in sin, and after he is dead can have another probation, another chance to repent, that he may repent after his death and turn to God and be saved. The Old Book does not hold out any such hope. That

kind of teaching contradicts the plain teaching of the Word of God, which says distinctly that " the deeds done in the body," in the life that now is, are to determine the issues of Eternity.

That man to-night who is living in drunkenness, who is squandering his time, squandering his money, squandering his manhood in a life of dissipation; you will have to answer for it in that day. That woman to-night who is living a life of frivolity and pleasure instead of living for the God who made her, and the Christ who died for her; you will have to answer for it in that day. That man here who professes to be a Christian but lives like the world; you will have to answer for it in that day. That man who has made gold his god, overreaching his neighbour in business, oppressing his employee, turning a deaf ear to the cry of the widow and orphan; you will have to answer for it in that day. That man who knows the truth but will not heed it because it will hurt him in business or politics; you will have to answer for it in that day. That man who is a libertine, living in lust, living like a beast, scattering ruin wherever he goes; you will have to answer for it in that day. The deeds done in the body—they will all come up, things that have been forgotten for years. There is a man here who years ago did a base, nefarious deed, and to-night he is very comfortable in the thought that no one on earth knows of it. Man, the whole world will know about it in that day unless you repent, and Jesus Christ will know about it, and will pass judgment upon it. There is a woman here to-night who has a very black page in her past history, but of late years she has been very comfortable over that black page. No one now knows anything about it; it is all forgotten; there is no one to bring it up. The whole world will know about it in that day unless you repent and turn to Christ.

2. "The secret things" will be judged. In Romans ii. 16, we read: "In the day when God shall judge the secrets of men by Jesus Christ." The secret things, the things done in the dark, the things done under the cover of night, the things that nobody saw but God; all will be brought to light on that day.

I remember hearing years ago of an incident that happened here, in your own country. A woman had killed her husband by driving a nail into his skull, and so successfully had she covered up the wound that he was buried without any suspicion being cast upon her. After several years the woman flattered herself that she would never be found out. One day, however, the grave-digger was at work in the cemetery, and threw up this man's skull, and there he saw the nail. I do not know that he suspected the woman, but he took it to her, and said, "Look there." She threw up her hands and cried, "My God! Found out at last." It will all be found out at last, the secret things, the thoughts and imaginations of the heart. Oh, you men who are boasting of your morality, how would you like to have the thoughts and fancies and desires and the imaginations of the last twenty-four hours photographed and thrown upon a screen before this audience to-night? The whole world will see those secret things in that day, not those of twenty-four hours

only, but those of a lifetime, unless you repent.
You, madam, who have boasted of your purity and
your nobility of character above others, and fancied
that you ought to be saved because of your goodness; how would you like to have the hidden things
of the chambers of imagery and imagination and
desire photographed and thrown on a screen before
all this audience ? But the whole world will see it
in that day, unless you repent. The secret things
will all come to light.

3. The Lord tells us again that the basis of
judgment will be. our *words*. In Matthew xii. 36 I
read, " But I say unto you that every idle word
that men shall speak, they shall give account
thereof in the day of judgment." Our careless,
thoughtless, unstudied words reveal what we are at
heart. Our studied speeches do not reveal what we
are, but what we would like to be; but our idle words,
that we drop accidentally, they are the best revelation of what there is in our hearts. Your impure
words, your unkind words, your harsh words, your
words of gossip and slander; you will give account
thereof.

On one occasion, at a service in Minneapolis, one
of my workers came to me and said, " Here is an
infidel; will you come and speak to him ?"   I
went to him, and in reply to my question he said
" Yes, I am an infidel." I said " Why are you an
infidel ? " He replied " Because the Bible is full of
contradictions."   " Full of contradictions ? " I said.
" Yes," he said.   " Will you please show me one ? "
I asked.   " Oh," said he, " it is full of them."   " Well,"
I said, " if there are so many you ought to be able

to show me one." "Oh, it is just full of them," he said. "Well," I insisted, "please show me one." Then he replied, "Well, I don't pretend to know as much about the Bible as you do." I said, "Then what are you talking about it for in this way?" Then I looked him right square in the eye, and I told him what Jesus said of the idle words that men speak. "Now," I said, "this is God's Word. God is the author of this book, and you lightly and thoughtlessly have been slandering the Word of God, and thus you have been slandering God, the author of it. I want to say to you, sir, that you will have to give account of your words in the day of judgment." The man turned pale, and well he might. I want to say to you men to-night that are pulling the Word of God to pieces because you have been told that some German scholar says so and so; you men that dare to criticise the Book you don't know anything about; you men that are taking up the idle talk of newspapers and reviews and retailing it, slandering God's Word, and God, the author of it; you will have to give an account thereof in the day of judgment. Well may you tremble. I want to say to you men who have taken the name of the glorious Son of God, in whom dwells all the fullness of the Godhead, lightly on your lips, and have been saying flippantly, "I don't believe that Jesus is divine, I don't believe that Jesus is the Son of God"; you men who have been robbing the glorious Son of God of what is His due, you will have to give an account of this in the day of judgment.

4. But the great basis of the judgment day

E

will be what we do with Jesus Christ. We are told in John iii. 18, 19, "He that believeth in Him is not condemned : but he that believeth not is condemned already, because he hath not believed in the name of the only-begotten Son of God." God has sent One down into this world to be our Saviour. He has sent His only Son. The rejection of Jesus Christ the Son of God, whom God has appointed to be our Saviour, our King, and our Lord, is the most daring and most damning of all sins. Light has been sent into the world, and men have loved darkness rather than light because their deeds are evil. There is nothing that reveals what is in the human heart so clearly as what a man does with Christ. Christ is God incarnate, the light of God come into the world ; and the rejection of Jesus Christ proves a wicked heart. The great question in the judgment day will be, "What did you do with Jesus Christ ?" Oh, I can imagine some people in that day. That man who sits in yonder gallery trying to make light of what I am saying to-night, he will be there ; I see him standing before the judgment bar, and the throng falls back, there is profound silence. Then comes rolling forth, like the sound of many waters, the majestic voice of the Judge, "What did you do with Jesus Christ ?"

IV. *The Judge.*—We now come to the fourth point. Who is to be the Judge in that day ? Jesus Christ Himself. "God hath appointed a day in the which He will judge the world in righteousness *by that Man whom He hath* ordained ; whereof He hath given assurance unto all men in that He hath raised Him from the dead." Jesus Christ is to be the Judge. That same Christ whom you are rejecting is to be the Judge. That same Christ whom you are robbing of the honour which is His due is to be the Judge. That same Christ whose divinity you are denying, not that you have any reason for denying it, but simply you don't want to have to believe it, and want comfort in your sin —that same Christ whom you are trampling under foot will sit as Judge in that day. That will be a very dark day for some people. It will be a dark day for Annas and Caiaphas, who robbed Jesus Christ of every form of justice. Now they stand before the bar, and Christ sits upon the throne. I can imagine Pontius Pilate in that day, who knew that Jesus Christ was innocent and yet condemned Him to appease the Jewish mob. Pilate will stand at the bar, and the Christ he so basely wronged will be on the throne. I can imagine the soldiers who spat upon Him, and mocked Him, and crowned Him with thorns. The Christ they spat upon, buffeted, and crowned with thorns, sits upon the throne, and they stand at the judgment bar. I can imagine Judas Iscariot, who for thirty pieces of silver sold his Master after three years of close association with Him; now he stands before the bar, and the Christ he betrayed sits upon the throne. I can imagine that man and woman in this audience to-night who have been telling their friends that they do not believe that Jesus is divine, who have been trampling the Son of God under foot, who have been resisting the invitations of mercy, it may be for years; you stand, before the throne, and the Christ whom you have defamed, slandered, rejected, and trampled under foot, sits as Judge.

V. *The Issues of the Judgment Day.*—Once more, please notice the issues of the judgment day. They will be eternal. They will be either eternal joy and life and glory, or eternal death, eternal darkness, eternal despair, and eternal shame. Oh ! men and women, I would that I had it in my power to-night so to picture to you that great judgment day, that every man and woman in this audience would go out from here with the judgment day of Christ before them as a great reality; but it surpasses my power. There is the judgment throne; its blazing glory, its overwhelming splendour, I cannot describe. There is the Christ upon the throne, His face shining with a glory above the glory of the noonday sun, His eyes like flames of fire piercing men through and through. And there you stand before that awful judgment bar, the eyes of Christ upon you like a flame of fire, piercing you through and through, your whole life laid bare, and your secret thoughts revealed.

Oh, men and women, repent, REPENT, REPENT ! " God now commandeth all men everywhere to repent, because He hath appointed a day in the which He will judge the world in righteousness by that Man whom He hath ordained; whereof He hath given assurance unto all man in that He hath raised Him from the dead."

Repent, REPENT, REPENT !

V

EVERY MAN'S NEED OF A REFUGE

"And a man shall be as an hiding-place from the wind and a covert from the tempest; as rivers of water in a dry place; as the shadow of a great rock in a weary land."—ISAIAH xxxii. 2.

I HAVE a very precious Old Testament text to-night —I love the Old Testament, it is full of Christ —Isaiah xxxii. 2: "And a man shall be as an hiding-place from the wind and a covert from the tempest; as rivers of water in a dry place; as the shadow of a great rock in a weary land."

A good many years ago I was travelling on the continent visiting some of the art galleries of Germany, and I saw a picture in the new art gallery in Munich that made a very deep impression on my mind. It represented the approach of a storm; the thunder clouds were rolling up thick and ominous; the trees were bending before the first approach of the oncoming tempest. Horses and cattle were scurrying across the fields in fright, and a little company of men, women, and children, with bowed forms, blanched faces, and terror depicted in every look and action, were running before the storm in search of a hiding-place. I do not suppose it was the artist's intention, but it has always seemed to me that this picture was an accurate representation of every human life. Every man and woman needs a hiding-place. You say a hiding-place from what? A hiding-place from four things.

I. *A Hiding - Place needed from an accusing Conscience.*—First of all, every one of us needs a hiding-place from the accusations of our own conscience. Every man and woman here to-night has a conscience, and every man and woman here to-night has sinned against their own conscience. There is no torment like the torment of an accusing conscience. We do not have to go to the Word of God to find that out. We find it in heathen literature as well. It was not a Christian poet, but a heathen of about the time of Christ, the Latin poet Juvenal, who said:

> " Trust me, no torture that the poets feign
> Can match the fierce, unutterable pain
> He feels, who, night and day, devoid of rest,
> Carries his own accuser in his breast."

It was another heathen poet, though he lived in a Christian land, the poet Lord Byron, who wrote:

> " Thus the dark in soul expire
> Or live like scorpion, girt with fire,
> Thus writhes the soul remorse hath riven,
> Unfit for earth, undoomed for heaven ;
> Darkness above, despair beneath,
> Around him gloom, within him death."

But we do not need to go to the poets to find out the torments of an accusing conscience. We find them round about us every day in actual life and experience. One night at the close of a service, at the church of which I am now pastor in Chicago, there came to me a woman with a haunted face and said, " I would like to see you in private." I replied, " If you will come to my office to-morrow at 2 P.M., I will have the pastor there; and if you have anything to say, we shall be glad to listen." The next day at two o'clock the woman came to my office, and Mr. Hyde, the pastor, was present; and I said to the woman, " Now what is the trouble ? " She made an effort to speak, and failed. Again I said, " What is the trouble ? " Now she made an effort, and again failed. For the third time I said, " What is the trouble ? We cannot help you unless you tell us your trouble." Then she gasped out, " I have killed a man. It was fourteen years ago, across the Atlantic Ocean in the Old Country, in the darkness of a forest, I drove a dagger into a man's throat, and dropped the dagger and ran away. He was found in the forest with the dagger by his side. Nobody suspected me, but everybody thought he had committed suicide. I stayed there two years, and nobody ever suspected me; but I knew I had done it, and was wretched, and at last I came to America to see if I could find peace here. First I went to New York and then came to Chicago, and I have been here twelve years, but have not found peace. I often go to the lake, and stand on the pier and look into the dark waters beneath, and I would jump in if I were not afraid of what may lie beyond death." Haunted and hunted by her own conscience for fourteen years ! Hell on earth ! Well, some one says, I can very readily see how a person who has committed so awful a deed as that, staining her hands with human blood, should be

haunted by her conscience. But I have never done
a thing like that.   That may be, but you have
sinned; and when conscience points at us the finger
of accusation, we do not so much balance up the,
greatness or the smallness of our sin.   But you say,
"My conscience does not trouble me."   That may
be, for it is a well-known psychological fact that
conscience sometimes sleeps; but conscience never
dies.   The day is coming when that sleeping conscience of yours will awaken, and your conscience
will point at you the finger of accusation, and woe
be to the man whose conscience wakes up, who has
no hiding-place from his own conscience.   In the
city of Toronto years ago there was a young girl
who had drifted there from the country.   She had
heard of the gaieties of the place, and had left her
home and come there for a life of pleasure, going to
theatres and dances, and amusements of that sort,
and like many another that goes to the great city
with the same object, she was caught in the mael-
strom of the city's sin, and had gone down, down,
down into a life of shame.   Her conscience did not
trouble her; but one night the Fisk Jubilee Singers
were singing in Toronto, and some friends asked the
girl to go and hear them, and she did.   At last they
came to that hymn with the weird refrain :

> "My mother once, my mother twice,
>   My mother she'll rejoice ;
> In heaven once, in heaven twice,
>   My mother she'll rejoice."

The poor girl was sitting up in the gallery, and as
she heard the strains of that chorus floating up to

her, all the memory of her childhood came back; she was a child, and at home again, in the old home. It was evening; the lamp stood upon the table, and her sweet-faced mother sat there with open Bible on her lap, and she a little girl of four, with golden hair, was kneeling at her mother's knee, learning to pray. It all came back again to her. Again the Jubilee Singers came to that refrain:

> " My mother once, my mother twice,
>   My mother she'll rejoice ;
>   In heaven once, in heaven twice,
>   My mother she'll rejoice."

And as those words came floating up again, the hot blood came to the girl's cheeks, she sprang to her feet, and rushed down the stairs out into the streets of the great city. On, on, on, as fast as her feet, now growing weary, could take her, out beyond the gaslights into the country; and next morning, when a certain farmer came to his farm-house door, there was the poor girl clutching the threshold, dead! Hunted to death by her own conscience.

Oh, there are men and women here to-night whose consciences are asleep, but whose consciences will some day awaken, and woe be to the man or woman whose conscience wakes up and who has no hiding-place from it.

II. *A Hiding-Place needed from the Power of Sin within Ourselves.*—In the second place, we need a hiding-place from the power of sin within ourselves. Now every man and woman here to-night who know themselves at all well know that there are powers of evil resident within themselves which are more than they can master in their own strength. If there is any man or woman who thinks that they have a complete mastery over themselves, if there is any man who thinks he has power to break away in his own strength from the sin that is within, he is a sadly deceived man. There are some people here to-night with the overmastering appetite for strong drink. Then there are others who do not care for it at all, but are enslaved by other sins. Others have a passion for gambling. Others care for neither of these, but have a love for other things. With another it is an ungovernable temper; with others it is a sharp, unkind, censorious tongue. With some it is one thing and with some another. But with every man and woman of us within these four walls there is the power of sin within ourselves, which is more than we can master in our own strength. We need a hiding-place from the power of sin within.

I remember one night a young man came to me at the close of a meeting like this, in Minneapolis, in America, and he said, " I heard you speaking in the street to-night, and I said to myself, ' that man can help me,' and I have come here and stayed through the service. Will you now help me ? " I said I would be very glad to do so if I could. He said, " Listen ; I was employed down in Pennsylvania, and I got to leading a fast life. Now," he said, " you know that a fast life costs money. It cost more than I earned, and I put my hand into my employer's money-till and took his money. Of course I was caught, but my employer was a good man. He might have sent me to prison ; instead of that he

said, 'You must go to the North-West. It is a
new country; begin life anew up there.' They sent
me here, and I have now got a good position, as you
see by my uniform," and he pointed to it. "But,"
he said, "I am going just the same way in Minneapolis that I went in Pennsylvania. I am afraid to
leave this hall to-night. Before I get a block from
this hall, I shall meet some one who knows me, and
just as sure as I do I am lost."

You may have no weakness in the direction that
this young man had, and again you may have; but
every man and woman here has the power of sin
within that is more than they can master in their
own strength. We need a hiding-place from the
power of sin within.

III. *A Hiding-Place needed from the Power of the
Devil.*—In the third place, we need a hiding-place
from the power of the devil. Over in our country
there are a great many people who are too wise to
believe in the existence of a personal devil. I
believe in the existence of a personal devil. I will
tell you why. In the first place, because the Old
Book says so, and I have found that the man who
believes in the Bible always comes out ahead in the
long run, and that the man who is too wise and too
advanced to believe the Word of God comes out
behind, in the long run, every time. Now, there
was a time when I was so wise that I believed so
much of the Bible as was wise enough to agree with
me. Thank God, that time has passed. Thank
God, He has opened my eyes and ears until I have
come to the place where I know—I wish I had time
to tell you how I know—that that Book, from the

first chapter to the last, is the very Word of God. Now,
this Book teaches us that there is a personal devil.
Turn to 1 St. Peter v. 8 : "Because your adversary
the devil, as a roaring lion, walketh about, seeking
whom he may devour."   Ephesians vi. 11, 12 : "Put
on the whole armour of God, that ye may be able to
stand against the wiles of the devil.   For we wrestle
not against flesh and blood, but against principalities,
against powers, against the rulers of the darkness of
this world, against spiritual wickedness in high places."
But, friends, there is another reason why I believe in
a personal devil, and that is, because of the teaching
of my own experience and my common-sense. Years
ago a great French man of science was crossing the
Arabian desert under the leadership of an Arab
guide.   When the sun was setting in the west,
the guide spread his praying-rug down upon the
ground and began to pray.   When he had finished,
the man of science stood looking at him with scorn,
and asked him what he was doing.   He said, "I am
praying." "Praying! praying to whom?" "To Allah,
to God."   The man of science said, "Did you ever see
God?"   "No."   "Did you ever hear God?"   "No."
"Did you ever put out your hands and touch God
and feel Him?"   "No."   "Then you are a great fool
to believe in a God you never saw, a God you never
heard, a God you never put out your hand and
touched."   The Arab guide said nothing.   They
retired for the night, rose early the next morning,
and a little before sunrise they went out from the
tent.   The man of science said to the Arab guide,
"There was a camel round this tent last night."
With a peculiar look in his eye, the Arab said,

" Did you see the camel ? " " No." " Did you hear
the camel ? " " No." " Did you put out your hand
and touch the camel ? " " No." " Well, you are a
strange man of science to believe in a camel you
never saw, a camel you never heard, a camel you
never put out your hands and touched." " Oh, but,"
said the other, " here are his footprints all around the
tent." Just then the sun was rising in all its oriental
splendour, and, with a graceful wave of his barbaric
hand, the guide said, " Behold the footprints of the
Creator, and know that there is a God." I think
the untutored savage had the best of the argument.
Friends, we see everywhere in this magnificent universe the footprints of the Creator. But, alas ! we
see everywhere in human society the footprints of
the enemy. Why, you have only to walk the streets
of London and you see the footprints of Satan ; you
see them in your dens of infamy, in the faces of
the men and women on the streets, and, alas ! alas !
you see the footprints of Satan in the homes of
culture and refinement. What means it that men
and women of education, men and women of refinement, fall under the power of all these strange de-
lusions, of Christian Science, Theosophy, and all that
sort of nonsense ? It means that there is a devil—
cunning, subtle, masterly, marvellous—more than a
match for you and me in cunning and power. We
need a hiding-place from the subtlety, the cunning,
the power, of the devil.

IV. *A Hiding-Place needed from the Wrath to come.*
—In the fourth place, we need a hiding-place from
the wrath to come. There are a great many people
who do not believe that there is " a wrath to come."

I do. Why? Again, because the Old Book says so. The Old Book says, as I showed you last night, that "God has appointed a day in the which He will judge the world in righteousness," and God has given assurance of this by raising Jesus Christ from the dead. The Old Book says: "There is to be a day of wrath and revelation of the righteous judgment of a holy and outraged God." I believe this because the Bible says so.

Another reason why I believe that there is "a wrath to come," is that my common-sense says so. Look here, here is a man who grows rich by over-reaching his neighbours, grows rich by robbing the widow and the orphan. He does it by legal means. Oh yes, he is too cunning to come within reach of the law. But he grows rich by making other people poor. He increases in wealth and is honoured and respected. When he goes down the streets in his magnificent equipage, the gentleman on the streets turns and says to his son: "There goes Mr. So-and-so, a man of rare business ability, a man who is now one of our leading men of capital. I hope, my boy, when you grow up you will be as successful as he." He lives in honour, dies in honour, dies respected by everybody—almost. And the victims of his rapacity, the victims of his oppression, the victims of his dishonesty lie yonder, bleaching in the potter's field, where they have gone prematurely because of his robbery. Do you mean to tell me that there will not be a day when these men who have lived on wealth wrung from the poor widow and orphan will not have to go before a righteous God and answer for it, and receive what they never

received in this world, the meet reward of their
dishonesty? Of course there is a judgment day;
of course there is a hell. If there is not, then there
ought to be. Look here, here is a man who goes
through life, never giving God one thought from
one year to another. He leaves God out of his
business, leaves God out of his social life, leaves
God out of his study, leaves God out of his pleasures, and makes God's day a day of pleasure, God's
book never opened, God's Son trampled under
foot. And thus the man lives, and thus he dies,
going through the world ignoring the God that
made him, and gave His Son to die upon the Cross
to save him. Do you mean to tell me that there will
not be a day when that man will have to go up
before a righteous God and answer these questions:
"What did you do with My day?" "What did
you do with My laws?" "What did you do with
My Word?" "What did you do, above all, with
My Son?" Of course there is a judgment day.
And you and I need a hiding-place from it, every
one of us, for every one of us has sinned and come
short of the glory of God. There are then these
four things from which we need a hiding-place—
our own conscience, the power of sin within, the
power and subtlety of the devil, and the wrath to
come.

Is there a hiding-place? I read my text again:
"A man shall be as an hiding-place from the wind
and a covert from the tempest, as rivers of water
in a dry place, as the shadow of a great rock in
a weary land." A *man* shall be—who is that man?
There is just one man that is a hiding-place—the

God-man, Jesus Christ. He is a hiding-place from
conscience. I have told you part of a story, and I
will now tell you the rest. When that woman came
and told me how she had been haunted by her
conscience for fourteen years, I took the Bible and
said to her, "Do you believe what is written in
this book?" She said, "Yes, sir, I believe it all.
I was brought up in the Lutheran Church." "All
right," I said, "listen" (Isaiah liii. 6): "'All we
like sheep have gone astray.'" I said, "Is that
true of you?" "Oh, sir," she said, "it is." "'We
have turned every one to his own way.'" "Is that
true of you?" "Oh yes, that is the trouble. It is
true." I said, "What are you?" She said, "I
am *lost*." "Very well, listen to the rest of it:
'And the Lord hath laid on Him the iniquity of
us all.' Now," I said, "who is the *Him*?" She
said, "It is Jesus Christ." "Well, listen: 'And
the Lord hath laid on *Jesus Christ* the iniquity of
us all.' Now," I said, "let my Bible represent
your sin, let my right hand represent you, and my
left hand Jesus Christ." I closed the Bible and
repeated the text: "All we like sheep have gone
astray. We have turned every one to his own
way." And I laid my Bible in my right hand and
said, "Where is your sin now?" She said, "It is
on me." "Well, listen: 'The Lord hath laid on
Him the iniquity of us all.'" And I laid the Bible
over on the other hand. "Where is your sin now?"
She hesitated and then said, "It is on Jesus Christ."
"Right!" I said. "Is it on you any longer, then?"
It was a few moments before she spoke, and then
she burst out with a cry of joy: "No, it is on Jesus

Christ !" That woman, who had been haunted by her conscience for fourteen years went from my office that day with the peace of God in her heart. Is there a man or a woman here haunted with the memory of the past? Christ is a hiding-place, and there is peace to-night for you in Him.

Christ is a hiding-place from sin within. I knew a young man belonging to a good family, highly educated, with noble aspirations, but completely overmastered by sin in one of its most loathsome forms. He tried to break away, tried to be a man, but failed, and he went down, deeper and deeper and deeper, until at last he was in despair and on the verge of a suicide's grave, and one awful night when despair had settled on his soul, he cried to God for Christ's sake, and Christ set him free. And never once did he fall into that sin again.

Thirdly, Christ is a hiding-place from the power of sin. I know a man in our home country—I think I never knew a man in my life more completely in the power of Satan than he was—a man of brilliant intellectual gifts, the most remarkable orator I ever heard. And yet he had gone down, and had fallen into the power of Satan, gone down until his friends had all left him, until his wife and children were wanderers, and he was a tramp on the streets. The man had gone down so low that on one occasion I was told he threw his poor wife down on the floor (one of the noblest women who ever stood by a fallen husband), and stamped on her with his heel. I said to him, "John, you ought to be repentant." He said, "Well, I don't believe as you do. I do not believe in God or in

F

your Bible." "But," I said, "John, that does not make any difference; if you will take Jesus Christ as your Saviour, He will save you, and if you do not take Him, you are lost." A few months afterwards, in another city, he went to his wretched garret, and threw himself upon Christ, and Jesus Christ met him and saved him and transformed him, and to-day he is one of the most honoured men in our land. There is no mere speculation about the religion of Jesus Christ. It is a present-day demonstrable reality. It is not merely that Christ saved people nineteen hundred years ago; he is saving them to-day in London.

Once more, Christ is a hiding-place from the wrath to come. Now, of course I cannot prove that from experience, for it lies in the future; but I can prove it by an argument that is un-answerable. That argument is this: the Christ that has power to save men from the power of sin now certainly has power to save them from the *consequences* of sin hereafter. Is not that a good argument? Let me add, that any religion that is not saving you from the power of sin to-day will not save you from the consequences of sin in eternity. There is a lot of religion in this world that is absolutely worthless. People tell you that they are Christians and that they are religious. They are saying their prayers, and doing all sorts of things. I will ask you a question: "Have you got that kind of faith in Jesus Christ that is saving you from the power of sin to-day?" If you have, you have that kind of faith in Jesus Christ that will save you from the consequences of sin hereafter. But if you have that kind of faith in Jesus Christ which after all is not faith, which is not saving you *now*, you have that kind of faith in Jesus Christ that won't save you from the penalty of sin hereafter.

Friends, Jesus Christ is a refuge, a hiding-place from conscience and its accusations, from the power of sin within, from the power of Satan, from the wrath to come, from all that man needs a hiding-place from. Who will come to this hiding-place to-night?

VI

THE DRAMA OF LIFE IN THREE ACTS

"A certain man had two sons."—LUKE XV. 11.

MY subject to-night is the Drama of Life in Three
Acts. The Lord Jesus Christ is the author of the
Drama, and it surpasses anything that was ever put
on the stage in conciseness, in point, in height and
depth, and fullness and beauty of meaning, in
pathos and in power. The Dramatis Personæ of
the drama are four—God, two men, and the Devil.
There are three Acts in the drama: the First Act,
Wandering; the Second Act, Desolation; and the
Third Act, The Wanderer's Return. There is a
Fourth Act, but with that we have nothing to do
to-night.

ACT I.—WANDERING ; OR, THE NATURE OF SIN

In the first act there are two scenes :

Scene 1.—A beautiful home, a spacious mansion,
with everything to meet every desire of the hearts
of its occupants. An aged father, whose countenance is full of nobility, and wisdom, and kindness, a
remarkable blending of strength and tenderness.
He is in earnest conversation with the younger of
his two sons. This younger son is tired of the
restraints of home. He has heard of the gaiety

in a distant country, and he longs to break the
trammels of his father's guardian care, and to see
the sights and enjoy the pleasures of this new land.
And he cries impatiently, " Father, give me the
portion of thy goods that falleth to me." A look
of inexpressible pain passes over the gentle face of
the aged father, but he grants the son's request.

Scene 2.—A leave-taking, a home-leaving. The
younger son has gathered all his property together,
got it into as portable a form as possible, and is
taking his journey to the far country. It is a
beautiful spring morning, the birds are singing
sweetly, the air is fragrant with the perfume of
spring flowers, the young man's voice is full of
gladness and good cheer, and with light and tripping step he wends his way down the avenue from
the old home, little thinking of the father who
watches him with moist eyes and lonely heart as
he leaves the front gate and goes out into a false
and cruel world.

In these two scenes we have a picture of the
nature, beginnings, and growth of sin. The father
in the drama is God; the son, man wandering
from God. The son wished to have his own way;
he was tired of the restraints of his father's control.
He desired to get away from his father that he
might do as he pleased. That is where sin begins—
in a desire to be independent of God, in a desire to
have our own way, in a desire to do as we please.
The essence of sin is in a desire to do what we
please, rather than be constantly looking to God
and asking Him what pleases Him. Is there any
man or woman here to-night who wishes to do as

they please ?   They have the beginnings of sin in
their heart.   Now, what you please to do may be
upright, may be moral, may be very refined, but
the desire to do your own will is the heart and
essence and substance of sin.   There are different
classes of sinners and different forms of sin.   There
is sin that is coarse and there is sin that is refined.
There is sin that is low and vulgar, and there is sin
that is genteel and elegant.   But all sin is alike in
essence.   It is man seeking to be independent of
God, man seeking to have his own way; that is
where sin begins, that is the very essence of sin.

The second scene represents to us the growth of
sin.   The son did not leave home at once.   His
heart was in the far country already, but he still
stayed at home.   But not very long.   Not many
days after, his feet followed where his heart had
already gone.   That is the story of sin in every
instance.   When a man starts out in the path of
sin, starts out to have his own way, he does not
give up all communion with God at once.   He
still goes to church occasionally, reads his Bible
occasionally, prays now and then, but less and less
as the days go by; until at last he begins to wonder
whether there is any God, begins to listen to voices
that say there is no God, and last of all, blatantly
cries, "No God, no divine Christ, no inspired
Bible, no God !"

How far have you got on that path of sin ?   Are
you just starting out ?   Are you seeking your own
pleasure, but still keeping up some form of communion with God, still attending the House of God
now and then, opening the Bible now and then

praying now and then, but less and less; or have you got farther down that road, down where you are never found in the House of God, never read your Bible, never go to God in prayer? Or have you got away off into the far country, where you say "There is no God, the Bible is not the Word of God, Jesus Christ is not the Son of God?" How far have you got down the path of sin?

Will you notice before we leave this Act that the father granted the younger son's request? He knew how the boy would use the money, but he also knew that the only way for him to learn wisdom was in the bitter school of experience. That is precisely the way that God deals with us. If a man desires to live independently of God, God lets him do it. God does not force a man into a life of communion with Himself, and conscious dependence on Himself; He gives us our choice and gives us our powers to make a living, and if we wish to live without communion with Him, He allows us to do it. If we can only learn the folly of living away from God by bitter experience, God lets us have the experience.

Act II.—Desolation; or, The Fruits of Sin

Scene 1.—It is a gay one. The young man has reached the far country, and life is one constant round of pleasure; balls, wine suppers, races, card parties, theatres, operas, all kinds of amusements, innocent and sinful, are the order of the day. Every day is a day of gaiety and every night a night of dissipation, and the young fellow is having a right royal time. Oftentimes he looks back on the quiet home life. Ah! how humdrum it was; how he pities his elder brother staying home there in all that dull life!

Scene 2.—The scene shifts. He is still in the city, but the boom has burst; hard times have come, men are out of work, famine stalks the street. On every corner there are little groups of men in ragged clothes, with pinched faces, with starvation looking out of their eyes, standing around trying to earn a chance penny by doing odd jobs, and our friend is among the company. "There arose a mighty famine in that land, and he began to be in want."

Scene 3.—A rural scene, but not a pleasant one. A great pasture, but not a blade of grass. In the prolonged drought every spear of grass has withered. In the midst of the field stands a lonely carob tree, from which hang the long pods covered with dust; a herd of gaunt, hungry swine are nosing about in the sand looking for stray carob beans. Our friend stands underneath the tree, looking eagerly up at the carob beans, for "he would fain have filled his belly with the husks that the swine did eat." At last, driven by hunger, but at the same time weakened by it, he wearily climbs the tree and shakes it till the pods fall from its branches; but the hogs have devoured them before he can reach the ground. Again and again he climbs the tree, but with the same result, and at last he falls upon the ground in despair, starving, "and no man gave unto him." In these scenes of the parable, we gave a picture of the fruits of sin. The first fruit

of sin is pleasure; the young man had a good time
at first.   There are those who tell us that there
is no pleasure in sin, but I will not tell you that;
first, because you would not believe me if I did.
You have tried sin and found pleasure in it.   I will
not tell you that there is no pleasure in sin, because
I know it is not true.   I tried sin and found
pleasure in it.   I will not tell you there is no
pleasure in sin, because the Bible does not say so.
It is true that the Bible says " there is no peace for
the wicked," and you know that is true, or, if you
don't know it now, you will before very long.   But the
Bible does not say that there is no pleasure in sin.
On the contrary, the Bible speaks in Hebrews xi.
of " the pleasures of sin."   Of course it adds that
they are only " for a season," very short lived.
There is pleasure in sin.   Some one has said, I
think it was Mark Guy Pearse, that the devil is
not such a fool as to go fishing without bait.   The
pleasures of sin are the devil's bait.   But, mind
you, the devil's bait always has a hook in it.   He
is dangling his bait before some of you here to-night.
" Oh," he says, " don't become a Christian; you will
have to give up this: the ball-room, look at this;
the theatre, look at this; the card party and its
pleasures, look at this."   And to-night, if you will
snatch the devil's bait, the first you know, you will
have the devil's hook in your gills, and you will be
on the bottom of the devil's boat, beneath a pitiless
sun, floating out over the sea of a hopeless eternity.

The second fruit of sin is want.   " He began to
be in want."   That is always the second result of
sin—want, famine, starvation.   Oftentimes they

come in a very literal form.   How many men there
are in London to-night without a decent coat to
their backs, without a meal in their stomachs, without a place to lay their heads, who once had plenty.
A friend of mine pointed out to me a man one
night in Chicago.   He said, " Do you see that poor
fellow there all curled up near the stove, with his
uncombed hair and ragged clothes ?   That man
used to be a Congress-man of this district."   Fast
times followed by hard times.   But it does not
always come that way.   There is many a man
living in sin who has plenty of money, plenty to
eat, plenty to drink, plenty to put on, plenty of all
material things; nevertheless want comes.   There
is other famine besides temporal famine.   There is
other starvation besides physical starvation.   A
man has a soul as well as a belly, though a good
many men in London live as if they did not believe
it ; but it is a fact.   The human soul is so large, so
vast, so glorious that God only can fill it, and away
from God there is starvation.   Augustine was right
when he said, " Thou, O Lord, hast made us for
thyself, and our soul is never satisfied until it
resteth in thyself."   Away from God there is
barrenness, away from God is an aching void, away
from God is the bottomless abyss of insatiable desire ;
away from God is woe, woe, woe !   Look at that
young fellow as he sits there in his tatters and with
uncombed hair, the hunger of his stomach looking
out of his half-crazy eyes, and see in that wretched
prodigal a picture of your soul, a picture of every
soul in this hall to-night that is away from God.

How well I remember a day and night in my

own life. I had started out one afternoon to have an afternoon and night of pleasure. With a little company of chosen companions I was in a hall that had been fitted up at great cost for pleasure. For a few moments I had left my gay companions, and I stood in the distance leaning against a pillar and looking at them yonder. And oh, there was such a cry, such an aching void, such a mysterious despair in my heart, that I leaned up against the pillar of that magnificent hall, and I groaned in the agony of my spirit. I was starving. What do you think I did? I shook it all off, and went right back to spend the afternoon and night as I had started out to spend it. What a fool I was!

The third fruit of sin is degradation and slavery. " He went and joined himself to a citizen of that country, and he sent him into his fields to feed swine; and he would fain have filled his belly with the husks that the swine did eat, and no man gave unto him." Jesus was speaking to Jews, and if there is any position low and degrading in the sight of a Jew it is that of a swine-herd. Christ meant this, that you and I have our choice between being God's sons, and hog-tenders to the devil. That is the choice open to every man here to-night. That young man might have been a son in his father's home, in glad, ennobling, and well-requited service, but instead of that he is hog-tender to a stranger. It is open to you to be a child of God in full and joyous surrender to His will, in glad and ennobling and well-requited service, or to be hog-tender to the devil. Men say, "I will not be a Christian. I want my own way." You cannot have it; no man

has his own way. It is either God's way or the
devil's. You can't have your own way—unless you
make God's way your own. Young man, which will
you choose to-night? To be a child of God, or to
be swine-herd for Satan?

Act III.—The Wanderer's Return; or, The Remedy for Sin

We come now to the third and last Act of the
drama. There are two scenes. The first scene is
the same lonely field. The young man sits beneath
the carob tree with his face in his hands and in despair. He begins to think. Visions of the old
home come before him. He sees his noble father;
he sees the well-laden table; he sees the well-fed
servants, and bitterly he cries, "How many hired
servants of my father's have bread enough and to
spare, and I (his son) perish with hunger!" and his
face sinks deeper into his hands. Then he lifts his
head with the light of a new hope in his eyes, and
he cries, "I will arise and go to my father, and will
say unto him, Father, I have sinned against Heaven
and before thee, and am no more worthy to be
called thy son: make me as one of thy hired servants. And he arose and came to his Father."
This is God's picture of the remedy for sin. Notice
what it is. In the first place he began to think—
that is where salvation begins, in *thinking*. People
say that Christianity is blind faith; not a bit of it.
Christianity is a rational faith that comes from
honest, candid, close thought. He began to think.
Men often say to me, "I am not a Christian, because
I think for myself." My dear friend, you are not a

Christian because you don't think for yourself. You don't think, and you know you don't. For every man who is not a Christian because he thinks for himself, I will show you a hundred who are not Christians because they don't and won't think for themselves. What is the trouble with you who are out of Christ? The simple trouble is that you won't think. You are bound not to think. You deliberately refuse to read every book that would make you think. You go down to hear some infidel lectures because you think that will prevent you thinking, because they stuff you with irrational nonsense. At a meeting like this, you will go out when the preaching becomes too pointed and you are compelled to think; some of you would do it now if you dared. If I could get you men and women who are out of Christ to think for thirty consecutive minutes, I would get you saved. The trouble is you are bound not to think. A stubborn refusal to think is sending tens of thousands of the men of Great Britain down to perdition.

He thought about the comparative lots of his father's servants, and of himself in this far country. The comparative positions of a child, or even a servant of God, and a servant of the devil; that is the thing to think about. I wish I could get a good and faithful servant of Christ and a faithful servant of the devil to stand together on this platform tonight, and just let you look at the two. Pick out the best servant of the devil you know in London, and then pick out the most faithful and devoted servant of Jesus Christ that you know; then make a call on them the same day, and study their faces. If this does not make a Christian of you, it is because you are not willing to give up sin. Compare the lot of the child of God, and that of the servant of the devil.

But, friends, he did not stop with thinking; his thought ripened into resolution. He said, " I will arise and go." It is not enough to think, you must resolve; there are people here to-night who have thought of this question often and who know just as well as I do that they ought to be Christians, but they never come to the point of resolution. In my first pastorate, there was one of our leading men in business and politics whom I know very well. I said to him, "John, you ought to be a Christian." " I know it," he replied. "I would give everything in the world, if I were a Christian. I know you have got the right of it, and the best of it, and I would like to be a Christian!" " Then," I said, " John, give me your hand on it, and take Jesus Christ right now." But he would never come to the point of resolution. Don't only think; resolve! What are you to resolve? " I will arise and go to the Father." That is the thing; come to God, to your Father. Come right to Him.

But notice how to come; come with a confession, and say "I have sinned." That is the only way a sinner can come to God—with a confession. God is willing to receive the vilest sinner on earth that will come with a confession on his lips.

The last step is " He arose and came to his Father." He turned his back on husks and hogs and hunger and turned his face towards home. Now we come to the last scene. The boy is nearing home. I don't know what his thoughts may have been by the way. He may have had doubts and

fears, he may have wondered how he would be
received, he may even have thought, "I wish I
could fix myself up better before going home."
But he had sense enough to come just as he was,
and he kept trudging right along on his journey,
and now he is within a few miles of home. Away
off yonder on the hilltop, as the sun is setting,
stands a man, an old man, in the last rays of the
setting sun, peering off into the west. He has
often been there before; it is the father looking
out into the west for the home-coming of the boy
that never came. The loving father is there again,
for love never wearies, looking out into the west.
Away down yonder towards the horizon he sees a
speck. Can it be the boy? It grows larger and
larger; it assumes the proportions and form of a
man, but not at all the boy who left his home; no
longer is it that rotund form, no longer is there the
bright glow of youth in his face, no longer is there
the light, tripping step. It is the figure of a man
prematurely old, with sunken cheeks and emaciated
form, clothed in rags and sore-footed, limping slowly
along the road. But those old eyes, though dim
with age, are sharp with love. Hear that cry,
"My son, my son!" The aged feet forget their
feebleness. The old man runs, and falls on the
neck of his son, and kisses him. The son begins to
stammer out his confession: "Father, I have sinned
against Heaven and before thee, and am no more
worthy to be called thy son." But the father won't
hear another word. He cries: "Bring forth the
best robe and put it on him; and put a ring on his
hand, and shoes on his feet; and bring hither the
fatted calf, and kill it; and let us eat, and be merry;

for this my son was dead, and is alive again; he was lost, and is found." Of what is this a picture? GOD—God's attitude towards the sinner. Although the son had forgotten the father, the father had never forgotten the son. For many years you have forgotten God, but God has never forgotten you. You have not thought of God for many a long day, but there has not been a day in which God has not thought of you, waiting to see some sign of your home-coming. If you turn your back on your sin to-night, if you turn your back on husks, hogs, and hunger, turn your face towards God; while you are still a great way off, God will run to meet you; and there will be the best robe of God's own righteousness in Christ to put on you, a ring for your finger, a pledge of your sonship; a kiss of reconciliation for your cheek, shoes of the preparation of the Gospel of Peace for your feet, and the fatted calf, typical of the great feast of joy and gladness in Jesus Christ. Men and women, come home to-night.

I heard years ago a story which I have never forgotten. A girl had gone astray, and had left her home for the great city. For some time she had continued to write to her mother, but after a while her letters became less frequent, and at last they ceased altogether. The mother suspected the worst, and came up to the city to search for the lost girl. She went to a gentleman who worked in the lower parts of the city, and asked him, "Can you get my daughter for me?" "Well," he replied, "I think I can, but you will have to do just what I tell you." "I will do anything to get my daughter," she replied. "Then," said the missionary, "go to a photographer and have your picture taken; have it taken large size, and have a hundred of them, and bring them to me." After a while, the mother came, bringing the hundred photographs. "Now," he said, "sit down and write underneath each photograph just these two words, 'Come home,'" and the mother sat down and wrote. "Now," said the missionary, "may I take these photographs down into the low parts of the city and put them up in the saloons and places of infamy?" It was a hard thing to ask of a pure woman, that her picture should be put up to the gaze of the outcast and the vile. But the mother's love said "Yes"—anything to win the girl. The man took them, and put them up in a hundred dens of infamy. Then he said to the mother, "Now go right home and wait." A few nights after, a group of revellers came into one of the places where the mother's picture hung; among the group was the lost daughter, who, looking across the saloon, saw that picture on the wall. It looked familiar. Stepping over to it, she saw in her mother's handwriting the two words "Come home." She knew what it meant; it broke her heart; she fled from the saloon, and took the first train for home, and in a few hours she was wrapped in her mother's arms.

That is what God has done in this fifteenth chapter of Luke. He has sent down a picture of Himself, a picture of His heart of love, of His love for you and me, and underneath it God has written, as it were in His own handwriting, these two words, "Come home."

Will you come to-night?

G

VII

A QUESTION THAT SHOULD STARTLE EVERY MAN WHO IS NOT A CHRISTIAN

"How shall we escape, if we neglect so great salvation?"—
HEBREWS ii. 3.

I HAVE a text to-night which I believe God has given me for this hour, a text that ought to startle every man and woman in this building who has not accepted the Gospel of Christ. You will find it in Hebrews ii. 3 : " How shall we escape, if we neglect so great salvation ? " I wish that that text would burn itself into the heart of every man and woman in this house who is out of Christ, " How shall I escape if I neglect so great salvation ? " I wish that every man and woman that may go away from this place to-night without definitely having received Christ as their Saviour and Lord and Master would hear it ringing in their ears as they go down the street, " How shall we escape if we neglect so great salvation ? " I wish that every one that may lie down to sleep to-night without a definite assurance of sins forgiven through the atoning blood of Jesus Christ, and of acceptance before God in Him, would hear it all through the night, " How shall we escape if we neglect so great salvation ? " Our text sets forth the folly and guilt of neglecting the salvation that

God has sent to us in and through His Son Jesus Christ, and that is my subject to-night. My sermon is all in the text—the folly and guilt of neglecting the salvation that God the Father has sent through His Son and in His Son Jesus Christ.

You notice I say not merely the folly but the guilt. There is many a man who thinks that perhaps it may be a foolish thing not to accept Christ, and admits the folly of it, but he has never realised the guilt of it. But I shall endeavour to show you to-night in the unfolding of this text that it is not merely an egregiously foolish thing, but that it is an appallingly wicked thing to neglect this salvation.

I. THE GREATNESS OF THE SALVATION.

We see the folly and guilt of neglecting this salvation, in the first place, by a consideration of the greatness of the salvation. " How shall we escape if we neglect so *great* salvation ? "

1. *We see the greatness of the salvation first of all in the way in which the salvation was given.* God sent His Son, His only Son, down into the world to proclaim this salvation, As we read in the preceding chapter, " God, who at sundry times and in divers manners spake in time past unto the fathers by the prophets, hath in these last days spoken unto us by His Son, whom He hath appointed heir of all things, by whom also He made the worlds ; who, being the brightness of His glory, and the express image of His person, and upholding all things by the word of His power, when He had by

Himself purged our sins, sat down on the right hand of the Majesty on high." Have you ever thought of it in the light of the context, that when God, in infinite condescension, the great and infinitely holy God, sent down His own Son to proclaim pardon to the vilest sinner, if you and I neglect this salvation we are pouring contempt upon the Son of God, and upon the Father that sent Him? If God had spoken this salvation by the lips only of inspired prophets, it would have a right to demand our attention. If God had gone above prophets, and had spoken this salvation by the lips of angels sent down from Heaven, it would have a still greater right to demand our attention. But when God, in His infinite condescension, sent not merely prophets or angels, but sent His own Son, the only begotten one, the express image of His person, God manifest in the flesh, to proclaim this salvation, and you and I do not heed it, we are guilty of the most appalling presumption and defiance of God. "He that despised Moses' law died without mercy under two or three witnesses," but how much sorer punishment you and I shall receive if we neglect this greater salvation.

2. In the second place, *the greatness of this salvation is seen in the way in which it was purchased.* This is a costly salvation. It was purchased by the shed blood, by the outpoured life, of the incarnate Son of God. Ah, friends, when God in wondrous love went to that extent that He sacrificed His very best, when God went to that extent that he gave His own and only Son to die on the cross at Calvary, that He might purchase your

salvation and mine, if you and I neglect so great salvation we are pouring contempt on the precious blood of the Son of God. "He that despised Moses' law died without mercy under two or three witnesses," but how much greater punishment shall he merit who tramples under foot the Son of God, and counts the blood of the covenant wherewith He was sanctified an unholy thing, and insults the Spirit of Grace (Hebrews x. 28, 29).

3. Again, *the greatness of this salvation is seen* in the third place *by a consideration of what it brings.* It brings pardon for all our sin, it brings deliverance from sin, it brings union with the Son of God in His resurrection life, it brings adoption into the family of God, it brings an inheritance incorruptible and undefiled, and that fadeth not away, laid up in store in Heaven for us, who are kept by the power of God, through faith, unto a salvation ready to be revealed in the last time. When you think that God has put at our disposal in Jesus Christ all His wealth, and is ready to make us heirs of God and joint-heirs with Jesus Christ, who can measure the guilt of neglecting and of turning a deaf ear to this wonderful salvation? Suppose that on his coronation day King Edward had ridden down to the East End of London, and seeing some wretched little boy on the street, clad in rags, with filthy face and hands, his great heart of love had gone out to that wretched boy, and he had stopped the royal carriage and said, "Bring that boy here," and they had brought the boy, and he had said, "I want to take you out of your poverty, out of your squalor and rags and wretched home;

I am going to take you to the royal palace and adopt you as my son." Then suppose the boy had turned and said, " Go along, I don't want to be adopted as your son; I would rather have my wretched crust of bread, I would rather have my rags and filthy home than live in your old palace; I don't want to go to be your son."

But when the great King of Glory, the King of Kings and Lord of Lords, the great Eternal Son of God, comes to you and me, in our filth and rags and sin, and wants to take us out of our filth and sin and rags of unrighteousness, and says, " I want to adopt you into my family and make you an heir of God and a joint-heir with Me," there are some of you men and women in this building to-night who, by your actions, are saying " Go away with your salvation, go away with your adoption into the family of God; I would rather have the crust of the world's pleasure and the rags of my sin than all the royal apparel of righteousness and glory which you offer me." Oh, the daring, damning guilt of any man or woman who neglects so great salvation !

II. THE ONLY SALVATION

A second thought which the text suggests is that our folly is great in neglecting this great salvation because it is the only salvation that is open to us. As Peter puts it in Acts iv. 12 : " There is none other name under Heaven given among men whereby we must be saved." It is salvation in Christ, or it is no salvation at all. A man is in a

burning building. If there were one way of escape
by a fire-escape, and another by a great broad stairway, he would have a perfect right to neglect the
fire-escape for the easier escape by the stairway. But
suppose there was no way of escape but the fire-
escape, how great would be his folly in neglecting
it. Men and women, you are in a burning building, in a doomed world. There is just one way of
escape; that is by Christ. In Christ any one can
be saved; out of Christ no one shall be saved. By
Christ, or not at all. There is a class of men to-
day who say, "Give up your Bible, give up your
Christ of the Bible," and we turn to them and say,
"What have you got to give us in place of our
Bible; what have you got to give us in place of
the Christ of our Bible?" Now we know by personal experience that the Bible and Christ bring
forgiveness of sins and peace of heart, for they
have brought them to us. We know that they
bring deliverance from sin's power, for they have
brought it to us. We know that they bring joy
unspeakable and full of glory, for they have brought
it to us. We know that they bring pardon
and a firm assurance of eternal life, for they have
brought them to us. We know that Christ makes
us sons of God, and if sons, then heirs of God, and
joint-heirs with Himself. What have you got that
will bring us the same, that will bring us pardon
and peace, and set us free from the power of sin?
What have you got that will bring us joy unspeakable and full of glory? What have you got that
will bring us the assurance of eternal life? Have
you anything? No, you have not. Well, then,

please, we are not quite so great fools as to give up
a book and a Saviour that bring us all these for
nothing. Salvation in Christ, or salvation not at
all. Point me to one saved man in London that
was not saved by Christ. I have been away round
this round earth. I have been in every latitude
and almost every longitude, north and [south; I
have talked with all kinds of people, of all races
and all classes, but I have never yet found a saved
man, who had a glad assurance of salvation and
practical deliverance from sin's power, that was not
saved by Jesus Christ; neither has anybody else.

III. To miss Salvation all that is Necessary is merely to Neglect it

In the third place, this text teaches us that to
miss this salvation, and to bring upon ourselves the
just and awful displeasure of a holy God for our
light and contemptuous treatment of a salvation so
wonderful, given and purchased at so great a cost,
all that is necessary is simply to neglect it. " How
shall we escape if we *neglect*—just neglect, so great
salvation ? In order to bring upon your head the
awful displeasure of God, and to be lost for ever, it
is not necessary that you go into any outrageous
immoralities; it is not necessary that you should be
an arrant and blatant blasphemer; it is not necessary
that you should abuse churches and preachers of the
Gospel; it is not necessary that you should even
positively refuse to accept Jesus Christ: all that
is necessary is that you simply neglect. More
people are lost in Christian lands by neglecting

than in any other way. There are millions in
England to-day who are going through life neglecting, drifting into their graves neglecting, drifting
into eternity neglecting, drifting into hell neglecting.
That is all that is necessary to be lost. Here is a
dying man, there stands a table by the dying man's
bedside, within easy reach, and standing on that table
there is a tumbler in which there is a medicine
that has power to save the dying man's life. The
man has strength enough to put out his hand and
take the tumbler and drink the medicine. Now
what is all that is necessary for that man to be
saved? All that is necessary is simply for him
to put out his hand and take the tumbler and drink
the medicine. What is all that is necessary for that
man to be lost and die? It is not necessary that
he should cut his throat or blow out his brains; it
is not necessary that he should throw the medicine out of the window; it is not necessary that he
should assault or insult the doctor or the nurse; it
is not necessary that he should positively refuse to
take the medicine: all that is necessary for that
man to die is to neglect to take the medicine.

Men and women out of Christ, you are dying.
Eternal death is at work in your souls to-night, but
on that table, in that Book, in the Christ of that
Book, there is a medicine that will save you, and
save you to-night if you will take it. The medicine is within the reach of anybody in this building.
Christ is nearer to you than the man or woman
that sits next to you in that pew. All you have
to do to-night to be saved is to put out your hand
and take Christ. "To as many as *received* Him to

them gave He power to become the sons of God."
What is all that is necessary to you to perish eter-
nally ? Not to commit moral suicide; not to commit to-night some awful act of immorality; not to
get up and curse Christ and the Bible; not loudly
to proclaim that you are an infidel; not to refuse
blatantly to take Christ: all that is necessary for
you to be lost is simply to neglect. Here is a boat
on the Niagara River, away above the Falls, towards
Lake Erie, where there is scarcely any current. A
man sits in the boat, being carried on very slowly
by the gentle current. There is a good pair of oars
in the boat, and the man could take them and pull
up the river towards the lake, or to either bank, if
he liked; but the man sits there and is carried on,
almost imperceptibly at first, and then faster and
faster, until, before he knows it, he is in the swift
current just upon the rapids, and he is being
carried on towards the Falls. The oars are no
good to him now, the current is too swift, he could
not save himself if he would; but on the shore
there are men who have seen his peril, they have
run along the bank and have thrown a line good
and strong. It falls right into the boat, at the
man's very feet. What is all that the man has to
do to be saved ? All he has to do is to lay hold of
the rope and they will pull him ashore, as has been
done more than once on that river. What is all
that he has to do to be lost ? It is not necessary
that he should take up the oars and pull with the
current; it is not necessary that he should throw
the oars overboard; it is not necessary that he himself should jump into the river: all that is neces-

sary is simply for him to neglect to lay hold of the
rope that lies before him, and the swift current of
the river will carry him on to absolutely certain
death over the cataract.

Men and women, that is a picture of every man
and woman in this building out of Christ. You
are in a boat in a perilous stream, being carried
towards the cataract of eternal perdition. There is
no man who has the power to take the oars in his
own strength and pull against that awful current;
there is no man on earth who can save himself;
but God has seen your peril, and, in the Gospel of
His Son, has thrown out a rope. It has fallen at
your feet to-night; all you have to do is to lay
hold, and He will pull you safely on to the glorious
shore. But what is all that you have to do to be
lost ? It is not necessary that you should jump
into the current or pull with the stream, or refuse
to accept Christ. All that is necessary is that you
simply *neglect*, and that awful current that you are
already in will sweep you over the cataract to
eternal death and ruin.

Some one put a little card into my hand one day,
a short, narrow card, and on the one side were these
words, "What must I do to be saved?" Underneath was written God's answer in Acts xvi. 31:
"Believe on the Lord Jesus Christ, and thou shalt
be saved." Then it said "Over," and I turned it
over. On the other side of the card was this question, "What must I do to be lost?" and there was
the answer in just one word: "Nothing." "Nothing!" You don't have to do anything to be lost.
You are lost already; if you do not do something

and do it quickly, you will be lost for ever. " How shall we escape if we neglect so great salvation ? " To sum it all up, friends, all that is necessary to be lost to-night, all that is necessary to bring upon our heads the awful wrath of God for our light and contemptuous treatment of a Gospel proclaimed by the lips of His own Son and purchased by the atoning death of His own Son, all that is necessary is simply to neglect.

Years ago in Minneapolis, the leading paper was the *Minneapolis Tribune*, published in a magnificent six or seven storey building, the finest newspaper building at that time in the North-West. I had occasion very frequently to go into the upper storeys of that building to see editorial friends. There was one great defect in that great building which I had never noticed. The defect was this, that the stairway went right round the elevator shaft, so that, if a fire broke out in the elevator shaft, escape by the stairway was cut off as well. There was, however, a fire-escape outside. That very thing happened. There broke out a fire in the elevator shaft, and it commenced to sweep up the shaft, storey by storey, cutting off escape by the elevator and cutting off escape by the stairway as well. But they had a brave elevator boy, who went up a number of times until he got a large number of men down from the upper storeys, and almost all the rest escaped by the fire-escape outside the building. But away up in the sixth storey there was a man, a despatcher for the Associated Press, which is the largest news-gathering agency in the United States. He was urged to escape, but he refused to move. There he sat by his instrument, telegraphing to all parts of the country that the building was on fire. He could have gone out of the building by the fire-escape, and across the road to an instrument there, and could have done just as well; but like a typical newspaper man, he wanted to do something sensational, and so there he sat telegraphing the news. There had been a similar case above Johnstown in the time of the Johnstown flood, when the dam of the river was breaking. A woman sat in a telegraph office at the bottom of the dam telegraphing down to the people at Johnstown that the dam was breaking, and that they had better flee for their lives. But she sat there, because duty required her, until the dam burst, and she was swept down in the flood. This man, however, sat there quite unnecessarily, merely because of his desire for notoriety. " I am in the *Tribune* building," he telegraphed, " in the sixth storey, and the building is on fire. The fire has now reached the second storey; I am in the sixth." In a little while he sent another message, " the fire has now reached the third storey." Soon he telegraphed, " the fire has reached the fourth storey; I am in the sixth." Soon again the message went over the wires, " the fire has reached the fifth storey ; I am in the sixth." Then he thought it was about time to leave ; but, in order to do this, he had to cross the hall-way to a window to reach the fire-escape. He went to his door and opened it, and, to his dismay, found that the fire had not only reached the fifth storey but the sixth storey, and that the hall-way was full of smoke and flame, which, the moment he opened the door, swept into the room. He shut the door quickly. What was he to do ?

The stairway, the elevator, and the fire-escape were all cut off; but he was a brave man, and he went to the window and threw it up. Down below stood a great crowd, six storeys down. There was no means of catching him if he jumped, and he stood there on the window-sill, not knowing what to do. But presently he looked up. Above his head was a long wire guy-rope that passed from the *Tribune* building to the roof of a building across an opening. Below him was a chasm six storeys deep, but he caught hold of the guy-rope, and began to go hand-over-hand across that chasm. The people down in the street looked on in breathless suspense. On and on he went, and then he stopped. The people below could hardly breathe. Would he let go? No. On and on he went, and again he stopped, and again the crowd below gasped, but only for a moment. His strength was gone, he was now obliged to let go, and down he came tumbling through those six storeys of space, crushed into a shapeless mass below. All through mere unnecessary neglect!

Men and women, you are in a burning building to-night, you are in a doomed world; but, thank God, there is a way of escape, and one way only, in Christ Jesus. No one knows how long that way will be left open. But, I beg of you, do not neglect it, and then when it is too late lay hold on some poor guy-rope of human philosophy, and go a little way, and then let go, and plunge, not six storeys down, but on and on and on through the awful unfathomable depths of the gulf of eternal despair. Men and women, turn to Christ to-night! "How shall we escape if we neglect so great salvation?"

VIII

A SOLEMN QUESTION FOR THOSE WHO ARE REJECTING CHRIST THAT THEY MAY OBTAIN THE WORLD

"What shall it profit a man, if he shall gain the whole world and lose his own soul?"—MARK viii. 36.

THAT question ought to set thinking every man and woman here to-night, who, because of love of the world, is refusing Jesus Christ.

I. Will you please notice in the first place the two things that are contrasted in the verse? The two things contrasted are not the present and the future. The question is not what shall it profit a man if he gain the present and lose the future. That would be an important question. If a man were to gain the fleeting present and thereby lose the eternal future, it would be a very foolish bargain; but that is not the question of the text. The man who loses his soul does not gain the present. It is true he loses the future, the eternal future; but he does not gain the present. The man living in sin, the man living away from Christ, does not get the most out of the life that now is. He gets the least out of it. On the other hand, the man that saves his soul does not lose the present. It is true that he gains the future, the eternal future; but he does not

lose the present. The man whose soul is saved gets
the most out of the life that now is. The two things
put in contrast are these, the world and the soul, or
life—the world, that is, the tangible world and all
it contains, wealth, honour, power, pleasure, everything that appeals to the senses, the lust of the
flesh and the lust of the eye, and the vainglory of
life (*cf.* 1 John ii. 16). That is the world. That
which is put into contrast with it is the soul or life,
the inner, real man. To gain the world is to get all
the wealth there is, and all the honour there is, and
all the social position there is, and all the power
there is, and all the worldly pleasure there is. To
lose the soul is to lose your real manhood, to fall
short of that for which God created you, to miss the
divine image, to have the divine image blotted out
and the image of the devil stamped in its place.

To lose the soul is to come short of the knowledge
of God, to lose communion with God and likeness
to God, to " fall short of the glory of God." Now
the question is this, What shall it profit you to gain
all that this world has, all its wealth, all its honour,
all its pleasures, all its power, and lose your true
selves, lose that for which God created you, lose
communion with God and likeness to God, and the
glory of God ?

II. For any man to gain the whole world at the
cost of forfeiting his soul would be a bad bargain.
If one could get the whole world by forfeiting his
soul, it would be an idiotic exchange. Why ?

1. *First of all, because the world does not satisfy.*
The world never satisfied a human soul. Take
wealth. Was ever any man satisfied with wealth ?

Did any amount of money ever bring satisfaction and lasting joy to any man or woman on earth? You had a man here in England a few years ago who was very successful in making money. He made millions of pounds sterling, but so little did it satisfy him that he jumped overboard from the deck of an ocean steamer and drowned himself. I remember one day that the heir to one of the largest fortunes in the world invited me to dinner, and I went to dinner with him. After the dinner was over he opened his heart to me, and confessed his dissatisfaction with life. All the millions—and there were a great many millions that that young man was heir to—did not give him satisfaction and joy.

Did honour ever satisfy any man? I have known men and women in the highest positions of honour in politics and social life, in culture and in all spheres of life, but I never knew a man or woman yet that was satisfied with honour. Does power satisfy any man? Was any king or emperor or czar, no matter how large his power, satisfied with the possession of power? Do the pleasures of life satisfy any man? Does the ball-room satisfy? Does the card party satisfy? Does the theatre satisfy? Does the race-course satisfy? Does gambling satisfy? Is there any form of the world's pleasure that satisfies the human soul? How mad then to forfeit your soul to gain money, honour, power, position, glory, pleasure, or anything that this world contains, when we know that they never satisfied anybody.

2. But *in the second place it is a mad bargain to forfeit your soul to gain the world, because the*

H

world does not last.   As the Apostle John says in
1 John ii. 17, " The world passeth away."   How well
we know it.   Take wealth.   How long does wealth
last ?   With many a man it does not last even a
few years.   A man is a millionaire to-day, and by a
turn of the wheel of fortune he is practically penniless to-morrow.   I was talking about a man of your
city only to-day to a friend of his, and he told me
how wealthy this man used to be.   But there was
a little change in the line of production in which
this man was interested, and your country ceased
to be the country that supplied that market, and
that man's fortune dwindled from millions to practically nothing.   I remember when I was a boy, one
night we five children were in the sitting-room at
home, and we asked our father to tell us what his
properties were.   We were going to figure them up
and see how much we were going to be worth when
he was gone.   He was rather amused at the idea,
and he began to tell us what he thought he was
worth ; and when he told us of all the possessions
he could think of, we all of us added them up, and
divided them by five to see how much each of us
would be worth when my father saw fit to hand
things over to us.   This looked splendid on paper,
and I felt quite rich that night ; but there came a
financial crash in America in 1873 which affected
my father's properties, and little by little, by the
year '77, when my father was called away, practically
the last vestige of all that he possessed was taken from
his hands, and he left only a few thousand dollars.
And that was mismanaged, and in a few months
not a penny was left.   All I had was a matchbox,

and a pair of sleeve-buttons, one of which I have
lost, and I don't know what became of the other!
"The world passeth away." I thank God that that
money did pass away. It was one of the best
things that ever happened to me.

Take honours. How long do they last? I remember a man in our country who stood pre-
eminent among the statesmen of America. I think
beyond all question he was the first statesman of
America of his day. He might have become
President, but he was a little too much of a
statesman to become President. England had an
unpleasant experience once with this man's states-
manship, when he represented the United States
Government at the Geneva Commission on the
Alabama claim, and carried the day. He was the
most highly honoured I think of any man of his
day in America, but after a while this man dropped
out, and we almost forgot there had been such a
man. I remember I was thinking of this man one
day, and I said to myself, "I guess So-and-so's
dead. I have not seen his name in the papers
at all lately," and a day or two afterwards I saw
in the papers that the Hon. So-and-so was living
in such a street of New York, that he never went
out in public, but sat by his open window looking
out upon the passing crowds and thinking of his
old-time successes. That man was utterly forgotten,
yet at one time he was almost the unquestioned
leader of political life in America. In a few months
more I took up the paper and read that he was
dead, and when he died there was nothing said.
He had dropped out of sight. Honour does not

last. Take your most honoured statesmen, whose names are in every mouth, no one will be speaking of them or thinking of them a few years hence. "The world passeth away." Suppose honour and money do last until a man dies. How long will they last? Twenty years, thirty years, forty years, possibly fifty or sixty years, and then—gone! One of our wealthiest men in America, the wealthiest man of his day, died. Two men on 'Change in this city, New York, met the next day, and one of them said to the other, "How much did So-and-so leave?" and the other one replied, "He left it all." So he did. Of his one hundred and ninety-six millions of dollars which he was worth, he didn't take one penny with him.

Pleasure, how long does it last? Take the ball; how long does the pleasure of the ballroom last? Somewhere from two to seven hours; then you go home with weary feet and throbbing brain, blaming yourself for having been such a fool. The card party: how long does it last? Oh, two or three hours, four or five hours; and then you go home with a lighter purse and a heavier heart. The champagne party; how long does it last? A few hours, and you go home with an aching head, a nauseated stomach, thinking what a fool you have been, and saying, "I will never be such a fool again." Ah friends, "the world passeth away."

The joys of friendship; how long do they last, if it is worldly friendship? A few brief years, and then we look into the casket on the beloved form and face, and the coffin-lid is locked down, and all is over. "The world passeth away." But the soul lasts. "He that doeth the will of the Lord abideth for ever." So I say that to forfeit your soul to gain the world is a mad bargain, for the world does not satisfy while you have it, and it does not last at all.

III. Now then, if any one here to-night could get the whole world as the price of selling his soul it would be a foolish bargain; but who ever got the whole world ? Who ever had all the world's wealth ? No one. The richest man has but a small portion of all the world's wealth. Who possesses all the world's honour ? The most honoured man on earth to-day has but a small portion of all the world's honour ? Who possesses all the world's pleasure ? The greatest devotee of pleasure has but a very small portion of all the world's pleasure. Who possesses all the world's power ? The mightiest man on earth has but a small portion of all the world's power. But even if you could get it all, it would be a bad bargain ; and what a mad bargain to sell your soul to get so small a portion of the world as any of you are getting !

I asked a man one night at a meeting like this— he looked a bright, intelligent fellow for a man of his class : " Why are you not a Christian ? " He replied, " I am deeply moved, and I would like to become a Christian. You have made me perfectly wretched. Yes, I would like to become a Christian." " Then why not become one to-night ? " He said, "My business forbids it. I would have to give up my position to-night if I became a Christian." I asked what was his business, and he replied, "A bar tender." He didn't look it ; he looked more respectable. I said, " Will you please tell me how much you get a week for tending the bar?" If I remember correctly it was six dollars, that is 24s.; and that man was selling his soul for 24s. a week. Some of you are selling your souls at almost as cheap a price. I asked another young fellow why he did not become a Christian. He said, " I believe in it, and I hope I may some day. But I am in a business of my own, and I have my best business on the Sabbath; I cannot be a Christian and do Sabbath work." Then I said, " You had better give up your Sabbath work." " No," he said, " I cannot do that. It is the biggest day's profit I have in the week." And that man was selling his soul for the profit of one day's business a week.

Why, there are some of you here to-night selling your immortal souls, for which Jesus Christ died, and which shall live for ever, in Heaven and glory, or in hell and shame, for some single form of pleasure. It may be the dance, it may be the card party, it may be the horse race, it may be the theatre, it may be some other form of pleasure to which you are a slave, and for one single form of worldly pleasure you are forfeiting your souls. Why, man, you are mad! " What shall it profit a man, if he gain the whole world and lose his own soul ? "

Friends, while I am talking here to-night, and offering Christ to you, and salvation in Him, all unseen but none the less present, there is another preacher here to-night, and that is Satan. He stands right by some of you as you sit in yonder pews, and while I offer you Christ and salvation and life eternal in Him, Satan offers you money, a little larger income in your business, or the social position that he tells you you will have to forfeit if you come out and out for Christ, or some form of worldly pleasure. He says, "Take this. Give me your souls and I will give you money. Give me your souls and I will give you these pleasures that you will have to give up if you become real Christians. Give me your souls and I will give you social position. Give me your souls and I will give you the world." Why, men and women, if he should offer you the whole world, you would be mad to accept his offer; but when he offers to you such a little trifle—the consummate folly of it—that for this little piece of the world you forfeit your soul; you forfeit life eternal for a world that never satisfies and does not last!

I have known many men and women that gave up the world for Christ, that gave up money for Christ, men that gave up much money for Christ, gave up high honour for Christ, gave up social position, high social position for Christ, gave up pleasures that had been the passion of a lifetime for Christ, but I have yet to find the first man or woman who regretted it, and I have known people who gave up Christ for the world, and when the hour came in which the eternal realities were opening upon them, they bitterly regretted it.

One day in New York City one of the wealthiest men that America ever produced, the first man that established a family name now famous, lay dying, with all his millions in the bank, and with all his railway stock of no use to him. And as he lay there, he said, "Bring in the gardener." The gardener was a godly man, and when he came in to see his dying master, the rich man said to the gardener, "Get down, and pray for me." The gardener did so, and when he had finished his prayer, the rich man said, "Sing,

> ' Come, ye sinners, poor and needy
> Weak and wounded, sick and sore.' "

Ah, men and women, a time is coming when we shall no longer see through eyes that are blinded by the glamour of this world ; the time is coming when every man and woman here to-night will have the scales taken from their eyes, and face to face with death, face to face with God, face to face with eternity, you will see as God sees. You will say, " What a fool I was to forfeit my never-dying soul to get the world that has not satisfied, and that is now slipping out of my grip." " What shall it profit a man, if he gain the whole world and lose his own soul ? "

A story is told of Rowland Hill, the great preacher. Lady Ann Erskine was passing by in her carriage, and she asked her coachman who that was that was drawing such a large assembly. He replied that it was Rowland Hill. " I have heard a good deal about him," she said ; " drive up near the crowd." Mr. Hill soon saw her, and saw that she belonged to the aristocracy. He suddenly stopped in the midst of his preaching, and said : " My friends, I have something for sale." His hearers were amazed. " Yes, I have something for sale ; it is the soul of Lady Ann Erskine. Is there any one here that will bid for her soul ? Ah, do I hear a bid ? Who bids ? Satan bids. Satan, what will you give for her soul ? ' I will give

riches, honour, and pleasure.' But stop! Do I
hear another bid? Yes, Jesus Christ bids. Jesus,
what will you give for her soul? 'I will give
eternal life.' Lady Ann Erskine you have heard the
two bids—which will you have?" And Lady Ann
Erskine fell down on her knees and cried out, " I
will have Jesus." Man and woman, two are bidding
for your soul to-night, Satan and Jesus. Satan
offers you the world, the world that does not
satisfy, and that does not last. Jesus offers you
life, real life, eternal life. To which will you listen?
" What shall it profit a man, if he gain the whole
world, and lose his own soul?"

IX

REFUGES OF LIES

"The hail shall sweep away the refuge of lies."—ISAIAH
xxviii. 17.

WE have seen in a former address that every man
needs a refuge from four things—from the accusations of his own conscience, from the power of sin
within, from the power of Satan, and from the wrath
to come. Almost every man has a refuge, that is,
he has something in which he has put his trust to
comfort him. The difficulty with most men is not
so much that they have not a refuge, as that they
have a false refuge, a refuge that will fail them in
the hour of crisis and need; what our text charac-
terises as "a refuge of lies." It was just so in
Isaiah's time; the men of Israel knew there was a
coming day of judgment, and that they needed a
hiding-place from that coming judgment of God,
and they made lies their refuge, and Isaiah—God's
messenger—proclaimed "the hail shall sweep away
your false refuge, the refuge of lies," and I come to
you with the same message, you men and women
that have a refuge, but a false one. "The hail
shall sweep away the refuge of lies."

I. How to Detect a Refuge of Lies

Is there any way in which we can tell a true refuge
from a false one, a refuge that will stand the test of
the coming day of God from a refuge that the hail
will sweep away ?   There are four tests that will com-
mend themselves to the reason and common-sense
of every intelligent and candid man here to-night,
whereby he can tell a true refuge from a false one,
a refuge that will save from a refuge that will ruin,
a refuge of truth from a refuge of lies.   The first
test is this :—

1. *A true Refuge is one that meets the highest Demands of your own Conscience.*—If that in which you
are trusting does not meet the highest demands of
your own conscience, it certainly is not a hiding-
place from the accusations of conscience.   Furthermore, it is not a hiding-place from the wrath of
God, for if our own hearts condemn us, God is greater
than our hearts, and knoweth all things.

2. The second test is this : *Every true Refuge is one,
trust in which is making you a better man or woman
to-day.*—If you are trusting in something which is
not making you a better man or woman to-day, it
is not a hiding-place from the power of sin within,
it is not a hiding-place from the power of Satan, it
is not a hiding-place from the wrath to come ; for a
refuge that does not save you from the power of
sin here on earth, very certainly will never save you
from the consequences of sin hereafter.

3. In the third place : *A true Refuge is one that will
stand the Test of the Dying Hour.*—If you are trusting
in something that simply brings you comfort when

you are well and strong, but will fail you in that
great hour that we have all got to face, when we lie
face to face with death and eternity, it is absolutely
worthless.

4. In the fourth place : *A true Refuge is one that
will stand the Test of the Judgment Day.*—If you are
trusting in something that will not stand the test of
that great Judgment Day, when we have to pass up
before the judgment bar of God to give an account of the deeds done in the body, it is absolutely
worthless.   There are men here in London indicted
for murders and about to be tried.   Now suppose
you went down to see one of these men, and you
found him in a very peaceful frame of mind, without a fear, and you said to him, " Well, you seem
very cheerful for a man charged with murder."
" Oh yes," he says, " I am ; I have no anxiety whatever about that trial."   And you say, " What, no
anxiety about it ? "   " No, none whatever," he replies.   " Why not," you say.   " Because," says he,
" I have an answer to make."   " Well, is your
answer one that will satisfy the judge and jury ? "
you ask.   " No," he replies, " I do not think it will
satisfy the judge and jury, but it satisfies me."
" Why," you would say, " what good is it if your
answer satisfies you, if it will not satisfy the judge
and jury before whom the case is to be tried."   The
question is not whether your hope satisfies you ;
will it satisfy God ?   I might add a fifth test : will it
stand the test of the Word of God ?

Here then are the four tests : first, Is it meeting
the highest demands of your own conscience ?
second, Is it making you a better man or woman ?

third, Will it stand the test of the dying hour?
fourth, Will it stand the test of the judgment day?

II. Refuges of Lies Examined and Exposed

Now we are going to apply these four tests to the
things in which men are trusting.

1. The first is *their own morality*.   How many
men in London there are, who, if you go up and
speak with them, and ask them to come to Christ,
say, "No, I will not come; I do not need Him."
You ask, "Why not?"   And they reply, "Because
I am a good man; my life and character are such
that I do not feel the need of a Saviour, and I am
trusting in my life and character to gain acceptance
before God."   Let us apply the tests.   You are
trusting in your own goodness.   Does your own
goodness meet the highest demands of your own
conscience?   Is there a man here to-night that
will say, "My life and character are such that they
meet the highest demands of my own conscience?"
Is there a man out of Christ here to-night who will say
that?   I have never met but two men who have
said it.   You will say, "They must have been remarkably good men."   No, they had remarkably poor
consciences.   The first one was a man I once met
while crossing the Atlantic Ocean.   I approached
him on the subject of becoming a Christian.   He
said, "I do not need any Saviour."   I said, "Do you
mean to tell me your life has been such, and your
character from childhood up to this moment, as to
satisfy the highest demands of your own conscience?"   He said, "Yes, they have."   But so

far from being an exceptionally good man, he was the most unpopular man on the boat before we reached New York City.

Second, Is trust in your own goodness making you a better man? As you go on from month to month and from year to year, do you find that you are growing more kind, more gentle, more self-sacrificing, more thoughtful of others, more considerate, more tender, more humble, more prayerful? Now I have known a great many men who trusted in their own goodness, but I have yet to meet the first one who, while trusting in his own goodness, grew better. As far as my experience goes, these men grow hard, grow censorious, grow harsh, grow selfish, grow more and more inconsiderate of others, grow more proud, and more bitter.

Third, Will it stand the test of the dying hour? Oh, how many a man has gone through life boasting of his morality, and trusting in his morality to save him in the life to come; but when that dread hour comes, when he lies upon his dying bed face to face with God and eternity, all his trust in his morality leaves him, in that illumination that comes to the soul as eternity draws nigh. I remember a man in one of my pastorates who was very, very self-confident. He had no use for the church, no use for the Bible, no use for Jesus Christ. He was very well satisfied that he was about the most exemplary man there was in the community, and he needed no Saviour. But the time came when there was a cancer eating into that man's brain. It was eating through the skin, eating through the flesh, it was eating into the skull, and eating so far into the skull that there was only a thin film left, and you could see the throbbing of the brain underneath. And when that man saw he had but a few days, and possibly but a few hours to live, his trust in his morality fled, and he said, " I wish you would go and call Mr. Torrey to come here and see me." I came to the bedside, and as he lay here in agony he said to me, " Tell me what to do to be saved ? " I sat down by that bed, and tried to show him from the Word of God what he must do to be saved. And as night came on I said to his family, " Do not sit up through the long hours of the night; I will stay up with him, and perform all that is necessary." And all through the hours of the night I sat beside that dying man's bed. Sometimes I had to go out of the room to get something for him, and whenever I came back there was always one groan from the bed over in the corner. It was this : " Oh, I wish I was a Christian ! I wish I was a Christian ! I wish I was a Christian ! " And so he died. His morality did not stand the test of the dying hour.

Will it stand the test of the Judgment Day, when you stand face to face with an infinitely holy God who knows you through and through ? Will you look up into His face and say, " O God, I stand here on my merits, on my character and life ! Thou knowest my life ; Thou knowest me through and through ; Thou knowest my every secret thought and act ; Thou knowest my life is pure, and I stand here before an infinitely holy God, and am proud of my morality."

Will it stand the test of God's Word ? Turn to Romans iii. 20 : " Therefore by the deeds of the

law there shall no flesh be justified in His sight."
Turn to Galatians iii. 10: "For as many as are of
the works of the law are under the curse: for it is
written, Cursed is every one that continueth not in
all things which are written in the Book of the Law
to do them."

2. There is a second refuge of lies, and that is,
trust in other people's badness. Some men trust in
their own goodness; other men trust in other folk's
badness. You go to them and talk about Christ,
and they say, "Well, I am just as good as other
folks. I am just as good as a lot of your professing
Christians." Oh, I know so many hypocrites in the
church. Instead of making their boast of, and
putting their trust in, their own goodness, they
make a boast of, and put their trust in, other
people's badness. Let us apply the tests. Does
that meet the highest demands of your conscience?
When your conscience comes to you with its lofty
demands, does it satisfy your conscience to say,
"Well, I am just as good as a great many professing
Christians?" If it does, you have a conscience of a
very low order. Is trust in other people's badness
making you a better man? Now I have known a
good many people, just as you have known them, who
were all the time talking about the badness of other
people. I have yet to meet the first one that grew
better by the process. Show me the man or woman
that is all the time dwelling upon the badness of
other people, and I will show you a man or woman
that is bad themselves, every time. Show me
the man that is always talking about another
man's adultery, and you show me a man that is an

adulterer himself. Show me the woman that is always having a suspicion about other women, and I will show you a woman you cannot trust. Show me a man that says every other man is dishonest, and I will show you a man who is a knave himself. I once had a Bible-class, and in that class there was a woman who was in business, one of those women who was always talking about the faults of others; and one day that woman propounded this question to me; she said, "Mr. Torrey, is it not true that every person in business is dishonest?" I looked at her and said, "When any person in business comes to me and asks if every one in business is not dishonest, they convict at least one person." She was angry, but I was only telling her the truth. Show me the man or woman who is always dwelling upon the faults of Christians, or the faults of anybody else, and I will show you a man or woman that is rotten to the core. I made that remark in my church when I was pastor in an American city, and at the close of the meeting a lady came and said to me, "I do not like what you said; you said, 'If you show me any man or woman that is always talking about the faults of others, you would show me some one that was bad.'" "Yes," I said, "and I mean it." "Well, there is Miss So-and-so. Now you must admit that she is always talking about the faults of others." I had to admit that this was a well-known fact. "You do not mean to say she is bad herself?" I did not answer, for I did not care to be personal; but if I had told her *all* the truth, I would have told her that that very week I had forbidden that very woman to sing in the choir any more because

I

of certain revelations of her character which had
been made to me, and to which she had confessed.

Will it stand the test of the dying hour ? When
you come to lie on your dying bed, will it give all the
comfort you need to be thinking about the faults of
others ? No. This very woman who accused every
person in business of being dishonest, who was always
dwelling upon the faults of others—the time came
for her to die; and as she lay dying, the doctor
came in, and said, " Mrs. So-and-so, it is my duty
to tell you that you must die." The woman shrieked,
" I cannot die; I won't die; I am not ready to die ";
but she did die.

Will it stand the test of the Judgment Day ? when
you go into the presence of God to answer to Him, will
you look up into His face with the same confidence
as you look into mine, and say, " O God, I do not
pretend to have been very good, but I was just as
good as a great many in the churches " ? Will you
do it, man ? Will you do it, woman ? Ah, the
blessed Book tells you, in Romans xiv. 12 : " So
then every one of us shall give account of *himself* to
God." Not an account of somebody else. In the
judgment day you will forget everybody but yourself. In that judgment day all other sin will vanish
but your sin.

3. The third refuge of lies is *Universalism*. There
are a great many men in every city, who, if you approach them on the subject of becoming Christians
and giving up sin, say, " Oh no, I will not do that;
I believe in a God of Love; I believe God is too
good to damn anybody. A man does not need to
forsake sin in order to take Christ. God is good,

and there is not any hell. Do you mean to tell me
God would permit a hell ; that a good God would
damn any one ? No, I do not need to forsake sin.
I am trusting in the goodness of God, and I believe
all men will at some time or other be saved." Now,
let us just try this. Does that meet the highest
demands of conscience ? when your conscience comes
to you and points out your sin and demands your
renunciation, does it satisfy your conscience to say,
" Yes, I am doing wrong, but God is so good I can
just as well go on sinning, I can just as well go on
trampling God's laws underfoot. He is so good He
will not punish me. He gave His Son to die for
me ; I can go on sinning as I please " ? Does that
satisfy your conscience ? Well, then, you have a
mighty mean conscience. What would you think
of a boy and girl, brother and sister, whose mother
lies sick in the house. The boy was sick a little
time before, and the mother had watched over him
so faithfully and tenderly that she had caught his
sickness ; she had brought him back to health, but
she was lying very sick and almost at the point of
death. She had told the children that they could
go out into the garden, and said, " There are some
flowers out there about which I am very careful. I
do not want you to pick them." So Johnny and
Mary go out, and Johnny goes to work to do just
what he was asked not to do. His sister expostulates,
and says, " Johnny, did not you hear mother tell us
not to pick those flowers, that they were very precious,
and that she did not want them picked ? " " Oh,
yes," says Johnny. " Then why pick them ? " asks
the sister. " Because," says Johnny, " she loves me

so, Mary. Don't you know how she loves me, how when I was sick mother gave up sleep and everything, and watched over me through the nights? Don't you know that she is sick there now because she loves me so? And so I am now going to do the very thing she told me not to do." What would you think of a boy like that, and what do you think of the man or woman that make their boast of the love of God, and because God loves them with such a wonderful love, make His love an excuse for sin, make God's love an excuse for rebellion against Him, make God's love a reason for a worldly and careless life? I should think you men and women would despise yourselves. Oh, the baseness of it; oh, the contemptible ingratitude of it; oh, the black-heartedness of it, making God's wondrous love, that gave Jesus to die on the Cross of Calvary, an excuse for sinning against Him!

Is your universalism making you a better man or woman? Oh, how many men grow careless, grow worldly, grow sinful, grow indifferent, because somebody has inoculated them with the pernicious error of eternal hope. How many men there are alive now, once earnest in the service of God, who are indifferent about the condition of the lost, the worldly, and the careless, because they have read some books undermining, or trying to undermine, the doctrines of Jesus and the Apostles. With what honeyed words the professing Church to-day is promulgating the doctrine of eternal hope, which is an infernal lie. Will it stand the test of the dying hour? Oftentimes it does not. Dr. Ichabod Spencer, one of the most able and faithful pastors America ever had, tells how, when pastor of a Presbyterian church in Brooklyn, he was called to see a young man who was dying. His wife and mother were members of the church, but this young man was not. The doctor went to see him, and tried to lead him to Christ ; but he turned and said, " It is no use ; I have had many chances, but I have put them all away and I am dying, and shall soon have to go ; it is no use talking to me now." And he was in great agony and distress of soul. Then the father came in and heard him talking and groaning, and he said, " My boy, there is no reason for you to take on so. There is no reason for you to feel so bad. You have not been a bad man ; you have nothing to fear." The dying young man turned round, and said to his father, " You are to blame for me being here. If I had listened to mother when she tried to lead me to a good life, instead of listening to you, I should not be in this strait. Mother tried to get me to go to Sunday school and to church, but you said God was so good it did not matter ; and when mother tried to take me to church, you took me fishing and hunting and pleasuring ; you told me there was not a hell, and I believed you ; you have deceived me up to this moment, father, but you can't deceive me any longer. I am dying and I am going to hell, and my blood is on your soul." Then he turned his face to the wall and died. Men, you turn people into sin by preaching a doctrine that contradicts the teaching of the Son of God. It means that you are deceiving the men you are rocking to sleep in sin, and they will live to curse you some day. And you men who are in health and strength are building upon a false hope. Death will tear away the veil that blinds your eyes to-night.

Will it stand the test of the judgment day? When you go up into the presence of God will you look up, and when He asks about your sin will you answer, "Yes, Father, I did sin; I did trample Thy laws under foot; I did neglect prayer, neglect the Bible, neglect the House of God, neglect obedience to Thee; I was worldly and careless, but I have a good answer. Father, my answer is this: I knew Thou wert a God of love, and gave Thy Son to die for me on the Cross of Calvary, and as I knew Thou wert so loving, I just went on trampling Thy laws under foot"? Will you do that? It won't stand the test.

4. A fourth refuge is *infidelity*. How many men there are, who, when asked to become Christians, turn and say, "I do not believe that the Bible is the Word of God. That is an old superstition that is worn out. I do not believe that Jesus of Nazareth was the Son of God. In fact, I am not quite sure that there is a God. I am not a Christian, and you can call me what you like. Call me an infidel, an agnostic, what you please; but I do not need any Christ, and do not believe in Him." He tries to comfort himself with infidelity. Hundreds of thousands are doing this in London to-night. Apply the tests. Does that meet the highest demands of your own conscience? When conscience asserts itself, and comes to you with its majestic demands, does it satisfy your conscience to say, "I do not believe in the Bible or in Jesus Christ; I do not believe

in God." Is your infidelity making you a better
man? I have yet to find the first man or woman
made better by infidelity. I have known men to
be made adulterers by infidelity; I have known
men and women to be made suicides by infidelity;
I have known men to be robbed of business in-
tegrity by infidelity; I have known men who were
made deceivers by infidelity and ran away from
their wives and went with other women. I could
stand here by the hour, and tell you of the characters I have known to be shipwrecked by infidelity.
I have yet to find the first man that was made
upright or moral or clean by infidelity. I stood up
one night in my church in Chicago. The church
was full, and a great many infidels were there. I
had invited them to be there, as I was talking
about " Infidelity; its Causes, Consequences, and
Cure." I stopped in my sermon and said, " I want
every man in this audience to-night that can
honestly testify before God and this audience that
he has been saved from drunkenness by the Gospel
of Jesus Christ to stand up;" and two or three
hundred men stood up, as having been saved from
drunkenness by the Gospel of Christ. I said, " That
will do. Now we are going to be fair, and give the
other side a chance, and I want to ask any infidel
in this audience to-night that has been saved from
drunkenness by infidelity in any form to stand up."
I looked round; at first I thought there wasn't any
one standing up. At last, away under the gallery,
I saw one, a very ragged-looking sort of a Sene-
gambian, and he was drunk at the time; that is an
actual fact. Thank God, he went down into the in-

quiry-room afterwards, and thought it over. Men and women, infidelity undermines character, infidelity robs men and women of purity, infidelity makes your clerks and cashiers unsafe. You know it.

Will your infidelity stand the test of the dying hour? A great deal of infidelity does not. A friend of mine who took part in the American Civil War, and fought for the North, told me a story about a man in his regiment who had been boasting in camp of his unbelief. On the second day of the battle of Pittsburg Landing, this man said to his comrades of his company, while waiting for the word of command to go forward, " I fear I am going to be shot this day; I have an awful feeling." " Oh, that's nonsense," they said, " it's just a pre- monition, a superstition, and there's nothing in it." Soon the command came, " Forward ! " and that company marched up the hill, and just as it went over the crest, there was a volley from the enemy's guns. The first one sent a bullet through his chest near his heart, and he fell back, and as they carried him to the rear, he cried, " O God, give me time to repent ! " It took only one bullet to take the in- fidelity out of him. It would take less than that to take the infidelity out of most of you here to-night. Will it stand the test of the judgment day ? Will you go up into God's presence, and when asked to answer for your sin, will you say, " Well, oh God, Thou knowest I did not quite be- lieve You existed ; I did not believe the Bible was Thy Word, and that Jesus Christ was Thy Son. I was an infidel ; that is my answer " ? Will you do this ? I will tell you how to try it. Go home to-night, and go down on your knees, and look up into God's face, and tell Him you are an infidel, and that you do not believe in Him, or in His Son, or in the Bible, and that you are willing to stand the judgment test. I went down in a meeting like this one night to the last row of seats at the back of the hall, and I said to a man there, "Are you a Christian?" "I should think not," he said, "I am an infidel." I said, "Do you mean to tell me you do not believe Jesus Christ is divine?" He said, "No, I do not." I said, "Just kneel down here and tell God that." He turned pale. And I say to you to-night who profess to be infidels, "Go and tell that to God alone, not when you are trying to brave it out in the presence of others but alone; meet God alone. Get down before Him, and tell Him what you tell me."

5. There is one more refuge of lies—religion. Religion is a refuge of lies. Religion never saved anybody. You say, "What do you mean?" I mean just what I say—religion never saved anybody. Trust in religion is one thing; trust in the personal Christ is another thing. There is many a man who trusts in his religion and yet he is not saved. You go to men, and they say, "Yes, I am religious; I go to church every Sunday; I read my prayer-book, and say prayers regularly every day; I read my Bible; I have been baptized; I have been confirmed or united to the Church; I have taken the Sacrament regularly, and that is what I am trusting in." Is it? then you are lost. Let us apply the tests. Does your religion satisfy the highest demands of your conscience? Does it satisfy your conscience,

when it points out your sin, to say " I go to church ;
I read the Bible ; I have been baptized and confirmed " ?   Does it really give your conscience
peace ?   Is your religion making you a better man
or woman ?   There is a great deal that is called
religion that does not make men and women better.
There is many a man who is very religious, and
goes to mass or to church every Sunday in the
year ; he goes to Confession very frequently, says
his prayers regularly, reads his Bible, and partakes
of the Communion ; he has been baptized, he has
been confirmed, and yet he is just as dishonest as
any other man in the community.   There is many
a man who is very religious, and yet oppresses his
employees in the matter of wages, or robs his servants in his home.   Many a most religious man is a
perfect knave.   Such religion will not save him, but
damn him with a deeper damnation.

Thirdly, will it stand the test of the dying hour ?
There is a great deal of religion that does not.
How many people have been very religious, and
yet when they come to die they tremble with fear.

Will it stand the test of the judgment day ?
Jesus Christ says it will not.   In Matthew vii. 22,
we read : " Many shall say unto Me in that day,
Lord, Lord, have we not prophesied in Thy name ?
and in Thy name cast out devils ? and in Thy name
done many wonderful works ? "—that is, they have
been very religious ; and Jesus says, " I will say unto
them I never knew you, depart from Me, ye that
work iniquity."   Friends, if you have nothing to
trust in but religion you are lost ; it is a refuge of
lies.

Well, then, is there any refuge ?   There is.   The
verse before my text gives it, Isaiah xxviii. 16 :
" Therefore thus saith the Lord God, Behold, I lay
in Zion for a foundation a stone, a tried stone, a
precious corner stone, a sure foundation."   That
foundation stone is Jesus Christ.   " Other foundation
can no man lay than that which is laid, *which is*
CHRIST JESUS."   As I said before, it is one thing to
trust in religion, and it is an entirely different thing
to trust in Christ.   Oh, friends, if your trust is in
Christ it will stand the test, it will meet the highest
demands of your conscience.   When my conscience
accuses me of sin, I say—

> Jesus paid my debt,
>   All the debt I owe;
> Sin had left a crimson stain,
>   He washed it white as snow.

He who had no sin was made sin for me, that I
might be made the righteousness of God in Him.
He Himself bore my sin in His own body on the
Cross "; and that satisfies the conscience.   The blood
of Jesus Christ gives the guilty conscience peace.
Trust in Jesus Christ makes me a better man.   It
has completely transformed my life, my outward life
and my inward life.   It will stand the test of the
dying hour.   Oh, how often I have gone to the
room of the dying man who was trusting in Jesus,
and he has looked up into my face with radiant confidence, without a tremor or fear, trusting in Jesus.
I remember one day I was told that one of the
former members of my Bible Class was dying, and
I went to his house.   I walked in and he sat there

propped up in bed. He was dying very fast. I said, " Mr. Pomeroy, they tell me you probably cannot live through the night." " No," he said ; " I suppose this day is my last." I said, " Are you afraid ? " He said, with a smile of perfect peace, " Not at all." I said, " Mr. Pomeroy, are you ready to go ? " He said, " I shall be glad to depart, and be with Jesus Christ." When Mr. Moody was facing the other world there was no fear. At six o'clock in the morning his son was by his bedside, and heard him whisper, " Earth is receding ; Heaven is open- ing ; God is calling." Then later, " Is this death ? This is not bad, this is bliss, this is glorious." Still later, some one began to cry to God to raise him from his bed of sickness, and he said, " No, do not ask that. This is my coronation day ; I have long been looking forward to it. Don't call me back ; God is calling me." Oh, friends, a living faith in Jesus Christ, the crucified and risen Saviour, will stand the test of the dying hour. It will stand the test of the judgment day. If it is the will of God, I am ready to go and meet Him at the judg- ment bar to-night, and when He asks me to answer, I have but one answer, the all-sufficient answer, " Jesus." That will satisfy God.

Throw away your refuges of lies to-night. The hail will soon come and sweep them away; " the hail shall sweep away the refuge of lies." Throw them away to-night. Take the only sure and true refuge, Jesus Christ.

X

THE WAY OF SALVATION MADE AS PLAIN AS DAY

"Then he called for a light, and sprang in, and came trembling, and fell down before Paul and Silas, and brought them out, and said, Sirs, what must I do to be saved? And they said, Believe on the Lord Jesus Christ and thou shalt be saved, and thy house."—Acts xvi. 29-31.

THE Philippian gaoler, by a train of circumstances, which I have read in the Scripture lesson to-night, had been brought to a realisation of the fact that he was a lost sinner, and had a deep yearning for salvation, and he put to Paul and Silas this direct question, "What must I do to be saved?" and Paul answered him in the words of the text, "Believe on the Lord Jesus Christ and thou shalt be saved." Nothing could be plainer, nothing could be more direct, nothing could be more positive than that. The way of salvation is to believe on the Lord Jesus Christ, and *the moment any man or woman or child really believes on the Lord Jesus Christ, they are saved.* If the most utterly lost man or woman in London should come into this hall to-night, and should here, or in the after meeting, or after they have gone out, believe on the Lord Jesus, the moment they did it they would be saved. Some

one may say, " But this was a word simply spoken
to one man ; what right have you to say that any
man will be saved the same way ? "   Because the
same thing is said over and over again in the Bible.
For instance, you read in Acts x. 43 : " To Him give
all the prophets witness that through His name,
whosoever believeth in Him shall receive remission
of sins." There isn't a man or woman in this building to-night that needs to go out of it without all
their sins being forgiven and blotted out. It is just
one act, " Believe on the Lord Jesus and thou shalt
be saved."

I.   What it Means to Believe on the Lord Jesus

What does it mean to believe on the Lord Jesus ?
We need to be very careful in our answer to that
question, for there are many answers to it that are
inaccurate and untrue.   There are men who say and
think that they believe on the Lord Jesus, and yet
they do not.   What does it mean to believe on
the Lord Jesus ?   I have given a very careful and
thorough study to this subject ; I have gone all
through my Bible looking up the word " believe,"
and all words related to it, and I have found out
what I suspected to be the fact when I began, viz.,
that " believe " means in the Bible just exactly
what it means in modern speech.   What is it
to believe on a man ?   To believe on a man
means to put confidence in him as what he claims
to be.   To believe on a physician means to put
confidence in him as a physician, resulting in

your placing your case in his hands.   To believe in
a teacher is to put your confidence in him as a
teacher, and accept what he teaches; to believe in
a banker means to put your confidence in him as a
banker, and to put your money in his bank.   And
to believe on the Lord Jesus means to put your
confidence in Him as what He claims to be.

To put confidence in the Lord Jesus as what?
As all that He claims to be, and all that He offers
Himself to be.   What does the Lord Jesus claim to
be, and what does He offer Himself to be?

1. In the first place, the Lord Jesus offers Himself to every one of us as *a Sin-bearer*.   In Matthew
xx. 28 He says, "The Son of Man came not to be
ministered unto, but to minister, and *to give His life
a ransom for many.*"   He offers Himself as a ransom
for all.   That thought runs all through the Bible,
in the Old Testament as well as in the New.   If
you want to find it in the Old Testament, turn to
Isaiah liii. 6 : "All we like sheep have gone astray;
we have turned every one to his own way; and the
Lord hath laid on Him (that is, on the Lord Jesus)
the iniquity of us all."   If you want to find it in
the New Testament turn to 1 Peter ii. 24 : "Who
His own self bare our sins in His own body on the
tree, that we, being dead to sins, should live unto
righteousness: by whose stripes ye were healed."
Christ offers Himself to every man as a Sin-bearer,
and to believe on the Lord Jesus is to put confidence
in Him as your Sin-bearer.

2. In the second place, the Lord Jesus offers
Himself to us as *a Deliverer from the power of sin.*
He says in John viii. 34, " Whosoever committeth

sin is the servant of sin." And we all know that is
true; for we have all committed sin, and become
the bond-servants of sin, and no man is able to
break away from sin in his own strength. He says,
in John viii. 36, "If the Son therefore shall make
you free, ye shall be free indeed." The Lord Jesus
offers Himself to each one of us as One who has
power to set us free from the power of sin. He
says that Satan is the strong man armed, but that
Himself is stronger than Satan. To believe on the
Lord Jesus is to put confidence in Jesus as One
who has power to set you free from sin.

3. In the third place, Christ offers Himself to us
as *a divinely taught and absolutely infallible Teacher*.
In John xiv. 10 He says, "Believe Me that I am in
the Father, and the Father in Me: or else believe
Me for the very works' sake. The words that I
speak unto you I speak not of Myself: but the
Father that dwelleth in Me, He doeth the works."
He offers Himself to you as the Teacher who speaks
to you the words of God, who speaks no words of
His own; as the Teacher who dwells in God, and in
whom God dwells, a divinely taught and absolutely
infallible Teacher; and to believe on Christ is to put
confidence in Him as such.

4. In the fourth place, the Lord Jesus offers Himself to us as *our Master, who has the right to the
entire control of our lives*. In John xv. 14 He says,
"Ye are My friends if ye do whatsoever I command you." To believe on the Lord Jesus is
to put confidence in Jesus as a Master who has
the right to have the entire and absolute control
of your life.

5. Again, the Lord Jesus Christ offers Himself to us as *a light and guide*. He says in John viii. 12, " I am the Light of the world ; he that followeth Me shall not walk in darkness, but shall have the Light of life." To believe on Jesus is to put confidence in Him as the Light of the world, as the One to follow wherever He leads.

6. And lastly, the Lord Jesus offers himself to us as our *Divine Lord*. He says in John xiii. 13 : " Ye call me Master and Lord : and ye say well ; for so I am." And we read in John xx. 28, 29, that when Thomas saw Jesus Christ after His resurrection, and was convinced at last that He really was raised from the dead, he threw up his hands and said to Jesus, " My Lord and my God ! " And Jesus commended Thomas for this confession, saying to him, " Thomas, because thou hast seen Me, thou hast believed : blessed are they who have not seen, and yet have believed." Jesus offers Himself to us as our divine Lord. To believe on Jesus is to put confidence in Him as our divine Lord.

So, to sum it all up, to believe on the Lord Jesus Christ is to put confidence in Him as your Sin-bearer, as your Deliverer from the power of sin, as your divinely taught and absolutely infallible Teacher, as your Master who has the right to the entire control of your life, as your Light and Guide whom you will follow wherever He leads, and as your divine Lord. The moment you thus put your confidence, your absolute confidence in Jesus Christ, that moment you are saved. " Believe on the Lord Jesus Christ and thou shalt be saved."

K

II. How Faith Manifests Itself

But how will we show our faith? In other words, if we really have believed on the Lord Jesus Christ and really have been saved, how will we show it?

1. In the first place, we will show it by *an assurance that our sins are all forgiven.* If I really put my trust in Jesus as my Sin-bearer, put my trust in Him as One who has borne all my sin, past, present, and future, the moment I put confidence in Him as that, I know I don't bear them any longer, and I have assurance that every sin I have ever committed is forgiven. In Luke vii. we read of a woman who was a sinner. She was an outcast. But she came into a house where Jesus was reclining at the table, and men thought Jesus could be no prophet because He allowed her to touch Him. But Jesus, when He saw her faith, said, "Thy sins are forgiven, thy faith hath saved thee; go in peace." When that woman went out of that place she knew that her sins were forgiven. If you had met her on the street and had said, "Do you know your sins are forgiven?" she would have said "Yes, I know it; I am sure of it." "Why are you sure?" "Because He told me so, and I therefore know it." "But do you feel it; do you feel as if your sins were forgiven?" Very likely she would reply, "I don't feel it yet; the news is so good I cannot realise it, but I am sure it is so; I know it, for He said so." "Well," you might have said, "you must not be so sure unless you feel it." And she would have replied, "Oh, I am *sure.*" But you

will say, "How can you be sure if you don't feel it?" And she would say, "Because He said so."

2. Secondly, if you have believed on the Lord Jesus Christ, it will show itself in your *looking to Him and trusting Him for victory over sin.* If you put confidence in Him as the Deliverer from the power of sin, you will certainly look to Him, and trust Him to set you free from the power of sin. You will not say, "My sins are so great that He cannot deliver me." You will not look at the greatness of your sin at all. You will look at the greatness of your Saviour.

A man came to me one day in Chicago, and said, "Mr. Torrey, I want to speak to you alone"; so I took him up to Mr. Moody's office—Mr. Moody was away at the time. He said, "I want to tell you my story." So I said "Very well; sit down"; and he began to tell me his life-story. He said: "Away over in Scotland, when I was but seven years of age, I started to read the Bible through" (a good thing for a boy to do) "and I got as far as Deuteronomy. Reading there I found that if a man kept the whole law for a hundred years, and then broke the law at any point, he was under a curse. Is that right?" I said, "Well, that is not an exact quotation, but it is about the substance of it." He continued, "I was only a boy of seven, but I was overwhelmed with the sense that I was under the curse of God, and that lasted for nearly a year. Then I got to the New Testament, and I read John iii. 16: "God so loved the world, that He gave His only begotten Son, that whosoever believeth in Him should not perish but

have everlasting life.' Then I saw that the Lord
Jesus had borne all my sin, and my burden rolled
away." He said, "Was I converted?" I replied,
"That sounds like an evangelical conversion." Then
he said, "Wait a moment; let me tell the rest of
my story. After some years I came to Chicago,
and I am now working down in the stockyards.
You know the stockyards neighbourhood; it is a
very hard neighbourhood. I have got into drinking
habits, and every little while I fall under the power
of strong drink. I try to break away, but I cannot.
What I have come to ask you is this, is there any
way to get victory over sin?" I said, "You have
come just to the right man; I can tell you that."
"I wish you would," he said. I opened my Bible
at 1 Corinthians xv., and I read the first four
verses: "Moreover, brethren, I declare unto you
the Gospel which I preached unto you, which also
ye have received, and wherein ye stand; By which
also ye are saved, if ye keep in memory what I
preached unto you, unless ye have believed in vain.
For I delivered unto you first of all that which I
also received, how that *Christ died for our sins*
according to the Scriptures; and that He was
buried, and that *He rose again* the third day
according to the Scriptures."

"Now," I said, "you believed that Jesus Christ
died for your sins." He said, "I did." "You found
peace in believing." "I did." I said, "But you only
believed half the Gospel, that Christ died for our
sins according to the Scriptures, and was buried.
Will you now believe the other half of the
Gospel? Will you believe that *He rose again?*"

He said, "I do believe; I believe everything that is in the Bible." I said again, "Do you really believe that Jesus rose again?" and he said, "I do." I said, "Do you believe what Jesus Christ says in Matthew xxviii. 18, "All power is given unto me in Heaven and on earth." "Yes." "Then He has got power to set you free from the power of sin. Do you believe it?" He said, "I do." I said, "Will you put your trust in Him right now, to do it?" He said, "I will." "All right," I said, "let us kneel down," and then I prayed, and he followed with a prayer something like this: "Oh God, I believed that Jesus died for my sins on the Cross, and I found peace through believing, and now I believe that Jesus rose again, and that He has all power in Heaven and on earth, and He has got power to set me free to-day. Lord Jesus, set me free from the power of drink and the power of sin." When he had prayed, I said to him, "Will you trust Him to do it?" He said, "I will," and he did. In a few weeks I received a letter from that man in which he said, "I am so glad I came over to see you. *It works!*"

Christ not only died, but He rose again, and is a living Saviour to-night. He has all power in Heaven and on earth, and the devil is no match for Him; the risen Christ has power to snap the fetters of strong drink, to snap the fetters of opium, to snap the fetters of lust, and of every sin; and if you will trust Him to do it for you, He will do it. To believe on the Lord Jesus Christ means to look to Him and trust Him to give you victory over sin.

3. In the third place, it will show itself in

your *unquestioning acceptance of the infallible and absolute truth and authority of everything Jesus says.*—If I put confidence in Jesus as a divinely taught and absolutely infallible Teacher, whatever I find in the Bible that Jesus says, I will believe it. I may not understand it, it may seem impossible, and the scholars may be against me, but I believe in the Lord Jesus, and what He says I accept absolutely in all its height, depth, length, and breadth. Many people to-day claim to believe in the Lord Jesus, but if they find Jesus teaching one thing, and men tell them that the consensus of the latest scholarship teaches something else, they accept the consensus of the latest scholarship, and throw overboard the teaching of Christ. Gentlemen, I affirm that those men do not believe in the Lord Jesus. They believe in " the consensus of the latest scholarship," and believing in the consensus of the latest scholarship never saved any one. It has ruined many. How can you say you believe in Jesus if you don't believe Him ? Belief in the Lord Jesus means to put confidence in Him, to put absolute confidence in Him as what He claims to be; and He claims to be a divinely taught Teacher, that speaks only the words of God.

It is a critical time in which we live, and the question is, shall we believe German scholarship so called, or the Lord Jesus Christ ? Well, in answer to that question, I say, the Lord Jesus Christ has stood for nineteen centuries, and German scholarship never stands for fifteen years consecutively; and I prefer to believe the Lord Jesus.

4. Our belief in Him will be shown by *studying*

His Word.—If I believe in the Lord Jesus, I shall
study His word over and over again. Suppose some
man should come to London claiming to be a
divinely taught and absolutely infallible teacher,
and that you believed in him. Would you not read
every word that he uttered ? We have a man in
America who claims not only to be a divinely taught
and absolutely infallible teacher, but a messenger sent
direct from God. Suppose I believed he really was
a teacher sent from God, I would study every word
he said, as hundreds do in Chicago. They spend
more time reading his words than they do reading
their Bibles. Just so, if I believe in Jesus as what
He claims to be, a divinely taught and absolutely
infallible Teacher, what I shall study above all else
will be the words of Jesus Himself.

5. Faith in the Lord Jesus Christ will show
itself by *a surrender of the entire life to His control.*—
If I put confidence in Jesus as what He claims
to be—my Lord, having right to the absolute control of my life—I will put my whole life in His
control. Have you done it ? You say you are a
Christian, you believe in the Lord Jesus Christ.
Are you proving it by putting your entire life in
His control ?

6. In the next place, you will show your belief
in the Lord Jesus Christ by *obedience to Him in
daily life, in whatever He tells you to do.*—In Luke
vi. 46 He says, " Why call ye Me Lord, Lord, and
do not the things which I say ? " I believe He is
saying the same thing to the Christians of London,
the professing Christians. You call Him "Lord, Lord,"
every Sabbath day in your lives, and then you go

through every day of the week living just as He
tells you not to live, and you refuse to do what He
plainly tells you to do. Now when the Lord Jesus
was here on earth and healed men, He demanded
faith as a condition precedent to healing, and He
demanded that they should show their faith by their
acts. He demands faith to-day as a condition precedent to salvation, and, having been saved, He
demands that you show your faith by your acts,
that you do what He tells you. That makes some
of you look very uncomfortable. I am glad of it;
it is a good sign. Some of you professed Christians
need to be brought under conviction of sin. You
have been praying that outsiders may be convicted
of sin, but a whole lot of you need to be convicted
of sin yourselves; and when *you* get convicted of sin
more of the outsiders will be convicted of sin.

7. Faith on the Lord Jesus Christ will show itself
again in *following Him wherever He leads.*—If I
put confidence in Jesus Christ as the Light of the
World, I will follow Him that I may "not walk in
darkness, but have the Light of Life." "He that
saith he abideth in Him ought himself so to walk
even as He walked." Are you following in His
steps, in your business, in your social life, in your
personal life, in your individual life everywhere?

8. Belief on the Lord Jesus Christ will show
itself in *confessing Him before the world, and in
witnessing for Him to men.*—We read in Romans x.
9, 10: "If thou shalt confess with thy mouth Jesus
as Lord, and shalt believe in thy heart that God
raised Him from the dead, thou shalt be saved.
For with the heart man believeth unto righteous-

ness; and with the mouth confession is made unto salvation."

I received a letter to-day from a man who said it was a very hard thing to expect people to stand up to confess Christ in the way I ask them to, and he went on to tell me an easier way to get at it. But I am not looking for an easier way. I abominate these easy ways. I believe in getting people converted. I could pass round cards and get them to sign their names, saying that they hoped to go to heaven; but a month after I had gone the effect would be nothing, or worse than nothing. I do not take any stock in any faith that does not lead to an open confession of Christ before the world, and I do not take any stock in the Christianity of your professed Christians unless it leads you to go out into the world and witness for the One who saved you. " Out of the abundance of the heart the mouth speaketh."

Now I put to you a question. Do you believe on the Lord Jesus Christ? You thought you did when you came in, but *do* you? I asked God in my prayer that He would sweep away false hopes to-night. Do you believe on the Lord Jesus Christ? It is one thing to say you believe, and another thing to believe. If you do not, will you believe on Him now, this moment? Will you put confidence in Jesus Christ this moment as your Sin-bearer, as a Deliverer from the power of sin, as a divinely taught and absolutely infallible Teacher, as the Lord who has the right to the absolute control of your life, as the Light of the World, as your Divine Lord? Will you do it? It takes but one instant to believe on the Lord Jesus Christ. It can be done in a moment. But it will take a whole lifetime to show that you have believed on Him after you have done it. The act of faith is instantaneous, the fruits of faith are life-long. Will you put your trust in Him to-night ? If you do, the results will follow, and if you never did it before, you can do it now. You can do it before Mr. Alexander sings.

And you men and women who never professed to believe in the Lord Jesus Christ, will you put your confidence in the Lord Jesus Christ now ? The moment you do it, you will be saved. I will tell any man or woman who is utterly unsaved, that in the next moment you may be saved. I will tell any man or woman who is utterly unsaved, who wishes to flee from underneath the wrath of God and come underneath the full sunlight of God's favour, that you can do it in an instant. How ? Believe on the Lord Jesus Christ; put confidence in the Lord Jesus Christ as what He claims to be. If the vilest outcast in London should be in this room now and should here and now put confidence in Jesus as all He claims to be, the moment he did it God would blot out all his sin, and set to his account all the righteousness of Christ ; and set him free from the power of sin, and transform him into a child of God. Old things in a moment would pass away and all things would become new. Oh the miracle of regeneration ! I have seen a man one moment a drunkard, half drunk at the time, get his eyes open enough to see the truth about the Lord Jesus and put his trust in Him, and the next moment I was looking into the eyes of a child of God.

One night in Chicago, in the Pacific Garden Mission, there came in a poor fellow, a complete physical and moral wreck. He had been in a railroad accident and was a total cripple, helpless on both feet, dragging himself along on crutches. For fourteen years he had been a victim of whisky and alcohol in all its forms, and of opium as well. He was an opium fiend and an alcohol fiend. My friend Colonel Clark spoke to him and told him the Gospel of Jesus Christ, but he refused to believe. But on La Salle Street, one of our busiest commercial streets, next day, Colonel Clark saw this same man dragging himself along on his crutches, and as he got to the entrance of an alley-way, Colonel Clark drew him into the alley-way and said to him, " My friend, Jesus has power to save you," and after talking to him a while, there and then the man got down as best he could on his crutches, beside the strong man of God, and put his trust in Jesus Christ. And when that man came out of that alley-way he came out a child of God, and he is to-day a preacher of the Gospel. Thank God for a Gospel that can save anybody. You cannot find me a man in all London that Jesus Christ has not power to save if he will only believe on Him. Put confidence in Him. Will you believe on the Lord Jesus Christ to-night ?

XI

WHAT IT COSTS NOT TO BE A CHRISTIAN

"I thought on my ways, and turned my feet unto Thy testimonies."—PSALM cxix. 59.

A GOOD many years ago I was talking to a young society lady in the city of New Haven in America, and suddenly she stopped me and said, " Don't talk that way; it makes me think, and I hate to think." The world is full of people who hate to think, and because they hate to think they go into things blindfolded, and come out with blighted hope and broken hearts and blasted lives. It is so in business. How many a business man there is in this city to-night who a few years ago had a business proposition made to him, and instead of sitting down, as any long-headed business man would do, and thinking it all over, and figuring it all out as to how much money he would have to put into that investment before he realised, how many years it would be before there was any adequate return, and what interest on his money there would be, just because it promised well on the surface he accepted the proposition without sufficient thought regarding it, he just put his money into that project and left it there, and that man's life ever since has been a wretched drag for a bare existence. Simply because he hated to think ! It is the same way in social life. How many a young woman has met at some social gathering a handsome, attractive young man, a young fellow of pleasant manners, who knows how to do the thousand and one little acts that mean so little and yet so easily gain the hearts of women, a young fellow who is a fine waltzer, and popular and attractive in all his ways; and one night that young man makes a proposal of marriage to her, and instead of sitting down, as any sensible girl would do, and asking herself whether that man has the mental and moral qualities that fit him to be a companion for life, just because he is handsome, because he is attractive and popular, because he is a beautiful waltzer, that young woman accepts his proposal of marriage and marries him; and a few months after she wakes up one day to find that she has married a fool, or, what is worse, a rascal. And all that woman's future life is wretched beyond description, just because she hated to think. But there is no place where that mistake is made so often and where it is so fatal as in the matter of being, or not being, a Christian. Men and women go into a Christless life, or, being in a Christless life, drift on in it, without even once sitting down to give the question thirty minutes' honest consideration, What it Costs to Live and Die without Jesus Christ. Now I am going to ask you to do some thinking to-night, some hard, serious, honest thinking. What I am going to ask you to think about is this: what it costs not to be a Christian, what it costs to live and die without Jesus Christ. And if when I get through you think you are willing to pay the price of a Christless life, I have nothing more to say. But if, when you have thought it all out, you come to the conclusion that it costs too much to live and die without Christ, I am going to ask you to do the only intelligent thing there is to do in the circumstances, that is, to stand up here to-night and declare your purpose to accept Jesus Christ right now.

What does it cost not to be a Christian? First of all, what is it to be a Christian? By a Christian, I understand, any man, woman, or child, that comes to God as a lost sinner, takes Jesus Christ as their personal Saviour, surrenders to Him as their Lord and Master, confesses Him as such publicly before the world, and strives to live to please Him in everything day by day. Let me repeat that definition. A Christian is any man, woman, or child, that comes to God as a lost sinner, takes Jesus Christ as their personal Saviour, surrenders to Him as their Lord and Master, confesses Him as such publicly before the world, and strives to live to please Him in everything day by day.

What does it cost not to do it?

1. In the first place, *not to be a Christian costs the sacrifice of peace.*—A Christian has peace: " Being justified by faith, *we have peace* with God through the Lord Jesus Christ."—Romans, v. 1. And having peace with God we have peace in our hearts, but no man out of Christ has peace. " There is no peace for the wicked, saith my God." One night in Chicago, after a meeting like this, when the congregation had gone out, I went and sat down in a seat by the side of a gentleman about thirty-five years of age, and I said, " My friend, why are you not a Christian ? " " Oh," he said, with a shrug

of his shoulders, " I am very well satisfied as I am."
I said, " You haven't peace." He said, " How do
you know that ? " I said, " Because God says so ;
' There is no peace for the wicked, saith my God.' "
The man dropped his head, and said, " You are
right, sir, I haven't peace." And there is not a
man or woman in this audience to-night out of
Christ that has peace. Money won't give you peace ;
the pleasures of this life won't give you peace ; no
number of good earthly friends will give you peace ;
not to be a Christian costs the sacrifice of peace.

2. In the second place, *not to be a Christian
costs the sacrifice of the highest, deepest, purest, holiest,
most overflowing joy that can be known right here on
earth.*—As we read in the Scripture lesson to-night,
in 1 Peter, i. 8 : " Though now ye see Him not,
yet believing in Him ye rejoice with joy unspeakable and full of glory." That was Peter's testimony. That is the experience of every true
Christian. A real living faith in Jesus Christ
gives a man joy unspeakable and full of glory.
Nobody out of Christ has joy unspeakable and full
of glory. " Oh," but you say, " I know many a
Christian that has not joy unspeakable and full of
glory." A real Christian ? You know there are
two kinds—professing Christians and real Christians.
Now I will admit that there are a great many people
in the world that call themselves Christians, who
have just enough religion to make themselves
miserable. They are holding to the world with one
hand, generally the right hand, and to Jesus Christ
with the other. Of course they have not joy
unspeakable and full of glory. But show me a

Christian who has dropped the world with both hands, and laid hold of Jesus Christ with both hands, and I will show you a man or woman that has joy unspeakable and full of glory, every time. But nobody out of Christ has joy unspeakable and full of glory. How Satan deceived me along that line for many years when I was a mere lad! I went one day up to the third storey of our home, where we had a great store-room where we put away the old books out of the library, and as a boy I loved to go and sit on the floor of that room, and get the books around me and look through them, and one day I came across the covenant of the church of my mother, and commenced to read it, and I said to myself, " I wonder if I cannot be a Christian ? " I can say " Yes " to that, and can say " Yes " to that, and that, and after a time I came to a place where it said something to this effect, " If I became a Christian I was to be willing to do anything God said, and go anywhere He said." I shut up the book and said, " No, just as likely as not I'll have to be a preacher if I say 'Yes' to that, and then life won't be worth living." And I threw that book away and deliberately refused to take Jesus Christ, and deliberately refused to think about it any more. Then I said to myself, " I am going in for all the pleasure I can get "; and I had a good opportunity to get it. My father was well off in this world's goods ; and as a boy of fifteen I was sent off to the university and matriculated for a degree, and my father sent me up all the money I wanted. Now, if you put a boy into a university, who learns easily and has no trouble to keep up with his class, a boy with

a rich father, who does not ask him how he spends
his money—I have often thought it would have
been a good thing for me if he had—if anybody
can have a good time, he can, and I went in for a
good time. Did I find it? You know whether I did or
not. I did not. And I went deeper, deeper, deeper,
deeper into dissipation and sin to find joy to satisfy
my unsatisfied heart.   I did not find it, and one awful
night, a mere boy still, with all hope gone, with life
desolate and bare, life so barren that there was
just one step between me and hell, in fact, that
very night I started to take that awful step, to
take my life by my own hand. I sprang out of
bed and drew open a drawer to take out the instrument that would end my life. For some reason or
other I could not find it.   God did not let me find
it, and I dropped upon my knees, and said, "O God,
if you will take this awful burden from my heart,
I will preach the Gospel;" and God not only re-
moved the burden, I found a joy I had never
dreamed of in this world, and all the years since it
has gone on increasing, with the exception of a
short time when I fell under the blighting power
of scepticism and agnosticism; all the rest of the
time all these years the joy has grown brighter,
brighter, brighter every year.   Young men and
women, if you want the deepest, sweetest, purest,
most overflowing joy there is to be known on earth,
come to Jesus Christ.

3. In the third place, *not to be a Christian costs
the sacrifice of hope*.   A Christian has hope.—As we
read in Titus i. 2, " In hope of eternal life, which
God, that cannot lie, promised."   Oh, how magnificent

L

that hope is, hope of eternal life ! How sure it is, resting on the Word of God, who cannot lie. The world has no hope like that. The world holds out no hope that has any foundation. Hope for the future is more important than present possession. " Oh," some one says, " I do not believe that; give me the present and I will let the future take care of itself." Yes, you do believe it. There is not a man or woman here to-night that does not believe that hope for the future is more important than present possession. A man says, " I do not believe it." Yes, you do ; I will prove it to you in five minutes. Suppose you had your choice to-night between being a millionaire and having all that money can buy for to-night, but no hope for to-morrow, but with the rising of to-morrow's sun and the opening of to-morrow's banks to be proved to be an embezzler, and all your money swept away, and you cast into prison to spend the rest of your life there ; or to be absolutely penniless to-night, but with the absolute certainty that with the rising of to-morrow's sun and the opening of to-morrow's banks you were to be a millionaire all the rest of your life, which would you choose ? " Oh ! " you say, " that's very easy ; I would choose to be penniless to-night, with the certainty that to-morrow and all the rest of my life I was to be a millionaire." So would I, but that only shows that you believe that hope for the future is more important than present possession ; and I would rather be the poorest child of God in the world to-night, with the absolute certainty that with the dawning of eternity I was to be for all eternity an heir of God and joint-heir with Jesus Christ, than to

be the richest man on earth to-night out of Christ,
with no outlook for all eternity but to be cast into
God's eternal prison-house of hell.   A man out of
Christ has no hope, even from the life that now is,
that is at all sure.   You say, "That is too strong;
a man out of Christ may have no hope for the
future, but if he is rich he has for the present life."
You are mistaken.   Come with me to New York
City.   We walk up Fifth Avenue; we stop before
one of the most elegant mansions there; we go up
the steps and are ushered through the hall down to
the library at the end of the hall.   You and I stand
there on the threshold and look into the library.
In it there are two men deep in earnest conversation.
This is not an imaginary case, but an actual one.   One
of these men is worth one hundred and ninety-six
millions of dollars, by an actual inventory of his
property taken a few days after the time of which
I am speaking.   The other man is one of America's
greatest financiers.   You and I stand there and look
in, and you say, "Well, I would like to be in that
man's shoes.   One hundred and ninety-six million
dollars !   I do not know anything about his religious
convictions, I do not know anything about his eternal
prospects, but he is well fixed for many years to
come so far as this life is concerned."   You are mistaken.   While you and I are looking in, that man
falls out of his chair on his face on the floor, and
when Quincey Garrett picks Wm. H. Vanderbilt
from the floor he is a corpse.   For all his one
hundred and ninety-six millions he had no hope
for five minutes.   Friends, we all of us here to-
night are like men standing on the seashore looking

out over the boundless ocean of eternity, and, as we look out, there come towards some of us—those of us who have a living faith in Jesus Christ— gallant vessels laden with gold and silver and precious stones, with every sail set, wafted swiftly towards us by the breezes of the divine favour. But toward the rest of us—those out of Christ— as we look out over the boundless ocean of eternity, there come no vessels, but dismantled wrecks, with no cargoes but the livid corpses of lost opportunities, over which are hovering the vultures of eternal despair, driven madly towards us by the fast-rising blasts of the indignation of a holy and an outraged God. That is what it costs not to be a Christian.

4. In the next place, *not to be a Christian costs the sacrifice of the highest manhood and the highest womanhood.*—Have you ever thought of it, that we have all fallen away from God's ideal of manhood and womanhood through sin ? Paul puts it in his tremendous way, " We have all sinned and *come short of the glory of God ;* " all fallen short of God's ideal of manhood ; and the only way back to it is by the acceptance of those regenerating and transforming powers that there are in Jesus Christ; or, to put it into ordinary language, by regeneration through Christ. And the best that any man or woman can attain to out of Christ is to be a mere caricature of manhood or womanhood as God created men and women to be. Is there a man in this audience tonight so lost to all that is noble, to all that is good, to all that is truly manly, that he is willing to be a mere caricature of manhood as God created man to be ? Is there a woman here to-night so lost to all

that is true, to all that is womanly, that she is willing
to be a mere caricature of womanhood as God created
woman to be ? That is what it costs not to be a
Christian; and, men and women, if there were no
other argument but that, I would come to Christ
to-night.

5. In the next place, *not to be a Christian costs
the sacrifice of God's favour.*——We have all sacrificed
God's favour through sin. The only way back to
God's favour is by the acceptance of the Sin-bearer
whom God has provided. How plain the Bible
makes that. Turn to John iii. 36: " He that
believeth on the Son hath everlasting life: and he
that believeth not the Son shall not see life; but
the wrath of God abideth on him." "Oh," but
some man says, " I do not know that I care about
that. The favour of God ? God is not real to me.
He is so far away. If I have the favour of my
neighbour, the favour of my employers, the favour
of my friends in the club, the favour of my con-
stituents in politics, I do not know that I care
whether I have the favour of this far-away being
that you call God, or not." Wait a moment ; when
you go out of this place to-night, look up at the
stars over your head, and say to yourself, " The
great God that made those stars, the great God
that made those wonderful worlds of light, about
which the astronomers are telling such wonderful
things in these days, the God that holds them in
the hollow of His hand as they go whirling through
space with such incredible momentum, that God loves
me, but He is displeased with me." When you
get home to-night and lie down to sleep, and can-

not—for I trust, in the kind mercy of God, some of
you will not sleep when you get home to-night
through thinking of what you have heard here—
when you get home and cannot sleep, and all the
rest of the house is asleep, and you lie there alone,
alone with God, looking up into the face of God, and
God looking down not into your face only but also
into your heart, say to yourself, " The great God into
whose face I am now looking up, and who is looking
down not into my face only but also into my heart,
that God loves me, but He is displeased with me."
Men and women, if I had to face that thought to-
night, if there were any way to find peace with God
—and thank God there is!—I would not rest till
I had found it.

6. In the next place, *not to be a Christian costs
the sacrifice of Christ's acknowledgment in the world
to come.*—How plain the Word of God is about that.
Turn to Jesus' own words in Matthew x. 32, 33:
" Whosoever therefore shall confess Me before men,
him will I confess also before My Father which is in
Heaven; but whosoever shall deny Me before men,
him will I also deny before My Father which is in
Heaven." You will often hear men say this: " If a
man believes in Christ in the secrecy of his heart,
even if he never confesses Him or says anything
about it, God yet knows what is in his heart, and will
accept him on the ground of the faith which he
never confesses." I challenge any man to show me
one line in this book that countenances such a
statement. That Word says as plainly as day, in
Romans x. 10, " For with the heart man believeth
unto righteousness; and *with the mouth confession is*

made unto salvation." That Word says as plainly as
day, and the Master Himself said it, in Mark viii. 38,
"Whosoever therefore shall be ashamed of Me and
of My words in this adulterous and sinful generation,
of him also shall the Son of Man be ashamed when
He cometh in the glory of His Father with the holy
angels." That word says as plainly as day, "Whosoever shall confess Me before men, him will I also
confess before My Father which is in Heaven, but
whosoever denieth Me before men, him will I also
deny before My Father which is in Heaven." You
say, "Does not faith save?" Yes, and faith confesses; and the faith that does not lead to confession
is no faith, and the faith that does not lead to confession will not lead to salvation. I can imagine
that great day, when the Lord Jesus summons all
His own before the bar of God. There we stand in
bright and glorious array, the Lord Jesus Christ at
our head, and He turns to His Father and says
"Father, all these are Mine; they confessed Me
upon earth before men, and I now confess them
before Thee My Father in Heaven." But look, away
over on the outskirts of that crowd is a man who
hung upon the outskirts of the Church of Christ on
earth. His sympathies were with the Church, his
associations were with the Church, but he was a
coward, and had not the courage of his convictions.
He was afraid of his business partner, of his as-
sociates in politics or in society, and he never
came out and confessed Christ openly before men.
But he thinks that because he hung upon the outskirts of the Church of Christ on earth, that he can
hang upon the outskirts up there. The Lord Jesus

Christ now turns to him—I do not believe it will be so much in anger as in unutterable pity—and with a sad wave of His hand He says, "Depart, depart; you did not confess Me upon earth before men; I cannot confess thee before My Father which is in Heaven." Men and women, that is what it costs not to be a Christian. Not to be an open, confessed, out-and-out follower of Jesus Christ.

7. Once more, *not to be a Christian costs the sacrifice of eternal life, and means to perish for ever.*—How plain the Word of God is about that. Take the words of Jesus Christ Himself in John iii. 14, 15, " And as Moses lifted up the serpent in the wilderness, even so must the Son of Man be lifted up: that whosoever believeth in Him should not perish, but have eternal life." How plain it is. Believe— have everlasting life; not believe—perish. John iii. 16: "For God so loved the world that He gave His only begotten Son, that whosoever believeth in Him should not perish, but have everlasting life." How plain it is; believe—have everlasting life; not believe —perish. Once more, John iii. 36: "He that believeth on the Son hath everlasting life: and he that believeth not the Son shall not see life; but the wrath of God abideth on him." How plain it is; believe— have everlasting life; not believe—"shall not see life; but the wrath of God abideth on him."

Do you ask me what eternal life means? I cannot tell you. I can tell you what its beginnings are, for, thank God, I have them in my own heart to-night. But what eternal life means in all its fulness, in its eternal outworkings, no human language can describe, and no human fancy can conceive.

I will tell you what to do. Take that moment of your life whose joy was purest, deepest, highest, holiest, divinest, multiply it by infinity, and carry it out to all eternity, and you will have some faint conception of what eternal life means. Do you ask me what it means to perish? I cannot tell you. You and I sometimes see the beginnings of it in the man or woman who have gone down through sin, in the depravity of their lives, in the corruption of their characters, in their wretchedness and despair. But what it means to perish in all the eternal out-workings of a depraved character, what it means to perish in that endless vista that lies ahead of us, no human language can describe, no human fancy can conceive. But I will tell you what to do. Take that moment in your own life whose degradation was deepest, whose corruption was completest, whose despair was the most blank and the most utter, and whose agony was the most appalling, multiply it by infinity, and carry it out to all eternity, and you have some faint conception of what it means to perish. And that is what it costs not to be a Christian.

Men and women, I put to you then this question: Are you willing to pay the price of a Christless life? If you are, I have nothing more to say. If not, I ask you to stand right up and profess your acceptance of Christ like men and women. Now I will admit that you may gain something by not becoming Christians. I will admit that it will cost you something to become real Christians. It will in all probability cost you the loss of friends that you hold very dear. I never knew a man to step out

of the world without losing friends. It will cost you
the loss of money, for real Christianity touches a
man's pocket-book. I am willing to admit that.
You cannot do some things in business if you become
a Christian that add to your income and which you
do to-day. I will admit that. I want you to know
this. I do not want you to come out under false
pretences. It will cost you very likely the loss of
pleasures of which you are very fond, and not for
one day only, but for weeks and months and years
to come. When I gave my heart to Christ I had
to give up everything I was most addicted to in the
days gone by, the things without which, it seemed
to me, life would not be worth living. I want you
to know this to-night. We want real conversion here.
But I also want to ask you a question : Are you willing, for the sake of a few godless companions that you
are better off without, are you willing, for the sake
of a few hundred or a few thousand or a hundred
thousand, if need be, of pounds sterling, are you
willing, for the sake of foolish, godless pleasures that
are unworthy of a thinking being anyhow, and
unworthy of your brain and your feet and hands,
that men and women ought to be ashamed of even
if they are not Christians, like the dance, the card-
table, the theatre, that intelligent people ought to
be ashamed of even if they are not Christians, are
you willing, for the sake of such things as these, to
sacrifice peace and joy and hope and manhood
and womanhood and God's favour and Christ's
acknowledgment and eternal life, and perish for
ever ? Are you willing to make so great a sacrifice
for so paltry gain ? One night in New York City,

at the close of a sermon by Dr. MacArthur, a gentleman came to him and said, " Dr. MacArthur, I want to ask you a question; if I become a Christian must I give up my money?" Dr. MacArthur was a wise man, and answered, "If you become a Christian, and Jesus Christ asks you for your money, you must be willing to give it up, every penny of it." The man said, "Dr. MacArthur, I will take a week to think about that." Dr. MacArthur knew it was no good pressing the man just then, and he said, "Very well." The man came back after a week, and said, "Dr. MacArthur, I have settled it; I will hold on to my money till death, and if Christ and Heaven must go, they must go." That was an awful decision, but it was an intelligent one. Are you ready to say that to-night? "I will hold on to my money till death; I will hold on to godless companions till death; I will hold on to my godless pleasures till death; and if Christ and Heaven must go, and peace and joy and hope and manhood and womanhood and God's favour and Christ's acknowledgment and eternal life must go, and eternal ruin come, let them go and let it come." Are you ready to say that, men and women? That is what you do say, practically, if you go out of this place to-night without Jesus Christ.

XII

THE MOST IMPORTANT QUESTION THAT ANY MAN EVER ASKED OR ANSWERED

"What shall I do then with Jesus which is called Christ?"— MATTHEW xxvii. 22.

You will remember that it was the Roman governor Pilate who asked this question, and he answered it wrongly, and brought eternal ruin and infamy down upon his own head. I trust that many in this great audience will answer it right to-night, and bring to themselves eternal life, eternal joy, and eternal glory. That question is the most important question that any man ever asked or answered, for if you do the right thing with Jesus Christ you will get everything that is worth having for time and for eternity; and if you do the wrong thing with Jesus Christ you will lose everything that is worth having for time and for eternity.

I.—SOME THINGS THAT DEPEND ON WHAT WE DO WITH JESUS CHRIST

I want to call your attention first of all to some of the things that depend on what we do with Jesus Christ.

1. In the first place, *our acceptance before God depends upon what we do with Jesus Christ.*——If you accept Jesus Christ God will accept you; if you reject Jesus Christ God will reject you. We read in John iii. 18 and 19: "He that believeth is not condemned, but he that believeth not is condemned already, because he hath not believed in the name of the only begotten Son of God; and this is the condemnation, that light is come into the world, and men loved darkness rather than light because their deeds were evil." Our acceptance before God does not depend on the good works we perform. In order to be accepted before God on the ground of our good works, our good works must be perfect; and no man's works are perfect. For it is written in the Law of God, "Cursed is every one that continueth not in all things which are written in the book of the Law, to do them;" and no one has kept the whole law, and therefore no man can be accepted on the ground of his works. Again, our acceptance before God does not depend on the character we have built up. In order to be accepted before God on the ground of character, our character must be absolutely holy, for God is an infinitely holy God; and there is no one who has not sinned.

Our acceptance before God depends upon our acceptance of Him who lived a perfectly holy life Himself, and then died as the substitute for those who have led unholy lives. If the vilest man or woman in London should come into this gathering to-night and should here and now accept Jesus as their Sin-bearer and Saviour, the moment they did it God would blot out every sin they ever committed, and their record would be as white in God's sight as that of the purest saint in Heaven.

I remember preaching one morning in my own church in Chicago on Romans viii. 1, " There is therefore now no condemnation to them which are in Christ Jesus ; " and I was led to make this remark : " If the wickedest woman in Chicago should come into Chicago Avenue Church this morning, and should here and now put her trust in Jesus Christ as her personal Saviour, the moment she did it God would blot out all her sins, and her record would be as white in God's sight as that of the purest woman in this building." Now quite unknown to me a true Christian woman, a member of my congregation, had gone out that morning, and had gone into one of the lowest dens of infamy in the city, and there she had asked a woman living in sin to come and hear me preach. But the woman answered " No, I never go to church; church is no place for a person like me." But the good woman replied, " Our church is ; the vilest sinner is welcomed at our church." " No, no," this outcast woman said, " I could never go." " But I will go with you." " No, that will never do," said the woman ; " the people on the street know me ; the policemen know me ; the very boys on the street know me, and sometimes they throw stones at me when I go down the street ; and if they saw you walking with me they would take you to be like me." But the lady replied, " I don't care what they think about me ; you come along with me, and I will go with you to the House of God." But the woman still refused, and said, "I cannot do that; but," she added, "you go a little way ahead, and I will follow you up the street." So the lady consented, and this woman who was a sinner followed her. They came to the corner where my church stands, and mounted up the steps at the entrance into the vestibule, and when they got inside the church, this poor woman who was a sinner dropped down into the very last seat, at the back of the church. I was preaching when she entered, and just as she got to that seat I uttered the words "If the wickedest woman in Chicago should come into Chicago Avenue Church this morning, and should here and now put her trust in Jesus Christ as her personal Saviour, the moment she did it God would blot out all her sins, and her record would be as white in God's sight as that of the purest woman in this building." My words went floating down over the heads of that audience, and dropped down into the heart of that woman. She believed it, and accepted Christ, and God met her and blotted out all her sins, and washed her record white, right then and there. And after that service the woman came down the aisle of the church to me, the tears streaming down her face, and told me how God had blessed her that morning.

2. In the second place, *our finding peace of conscience depends entirely on what we do with Jesus Christ.*—In Romans v. 1 we read, " Therefore being justified by faith, we have peace with God through our Lord Jesus Christ."

We can never get peace of conscience by good works ; we can never get peace of conscience by

prayers and penances. How many have tried to get
peace that way and have failed ! Martin Luther,
after his wild university life, roused to the sense of
the fact that he was a sinner, tried to find peace by
good works, by long nights of prayer, by penances,
but failed ! At last he went to Rome, and started
to climb up the steps at St. Peter's on his knees,
hoping to find peace that way, but failed. At last,
the words of God came ringing in his ears, " The
just shall live by faith," and Martin Luther put his
faith in the finished work of Christ, and found peace
instantly. I have a friend over in America, and in
the days before I made his acquaintance he was a
very vicious man. He was a professional gambler,
one of the most desperate gamblers on the Mississippi River in the old days of the Mississippi
gamblers. One night he was at the gaming table,
and a man across the table accused him of dishonesty at cards, and Stephen Holcombe, who is
now my friend, drew his revolver and shot at his
accuser. The bullet went into the man's neck, and
when he saw what he had done, Stephen Holcombe
sprang to the man's side, lifted his head on to his
knee, and tried to staunch the flow of blood in the
gaping wound ; but the man bled to death then and
there. Stephen Holcombe was arrested for murder ;
he was tried, and was acquitted on the ground that
he had shot the man in self-defence. But though
acquitted by a human court, he was not acquitted
before the bar of God, nor before the bar of his own
conscience. He tried every way to find peace. He
gave up gambling, and he gave up all his evil ways to
find peace, but he did not find it. He even united

himself to a church, and went to the Communion table, but he did not find peace. Two years after that awful night he was in his room alone in misery, his face buried in his hands, and the memory of that day was haunting him, and as he knelt there he cried : " O God, can anything blot out the awful memory of what I have done and give me peace ? " And the strains of the old familiar hymn came singing through his heart—

> What shall wash away my sin ?
> Nothing but the blood of Jesus ;
> What shall make me whole again ?
> Nothing but the blood of Jesus.

And then and there Stephen Holcombe saw Christ on the Cross for his sin. He saw all his sins, the murder and all, laid on Christ. Then and there Stephen Holcombe found peace, and from that day he has gone up and down our country preaching Christ and the atoning blood that gave him peace.

Is there some man or woman here to-night haunted with the memory of the evil you have done ? Men and women, there is a way to find peace, only one way—by simple faith in a Christ that was crucified on the Cross of Cavalry for your sin.

3. In the third place, *finding deep and abiding joy depends on what we do with Jesus Christ.*—As the Apostle Peter says in 1 Peter i. 8, " Though now ye see Him not, yet believing, ye rejoice with joy unspeakable and full of glory." A man can never get joy through the accumulation of wealth. Many have tried it, but no one has ever succeeded. A man cannot get joy through seeking the world's

M

honours; many have tried it, but no one has ever
succeeded. A man cannot get joy through indulging
in the world's pleasures; millions have tried it, but
no one has ever succeeded. But, friends, the
wretchedest heart in this world can find joy to-
night through believing in Christ crucified and
risen.

Some years ago I remember a noblewoman of
your country was studying at our Bible Institute
in Chicago, and on the day she left the Institute,
she told us these two incidents that happened over
here in England. She said, " I had a letter from
a dear friend of mine, a lady, and she asked me to
come at once to see her. I hurried to her home,
and, as I went up the elegant marble stairway
and saw the costly paintings on the walls and
the magnificent statues that lined the hall, I said
to myself, 'I wonder if all this wealth and splendour makes my friend happy.' I did not have
to wait long to find out, for presently the lady
came hurrying into the room, and, after greeting
me, dropped into a seat and burst into tears. All
the wealth, honour, and dignity of her position had
not given her joy. After this I went to visit a poor
blind woman in a humble cottage. It was a dark
rainy day, and the rain was dripping through the
badly thatched roof, gathering in a pool before the
chair where the woman sat. When I saw the
poverty of that blind woman, I was driven to turn
to her and say, 'Maggie, are you not miserable?'
'What, lady?' and she turned her sightless eyes to
me in surprise, 'What, lady? I miserable; I the
child of a King, and hurrying on to the mansion He

has gone to prepare for me? I miserable? No, no,
lady, I am happy!'" Wealth had not brought joy
to the one, but a living faith in Jesus Christ had
brought joy to the other in the midst of her poverty
and misfortune.

4. In the fourth place, *our obtaining eternal life
depends entirely on what we do with Jesus Christ.*—
We read in 1 John v. 11, 12, "God hath given to
us eternal life, and this life is in His Son. He that
hath the Son hath life; and he that hath not the
Son of God hath not life." What strange ideas
even Christian people have about how to obtain
eternal life. If I could come to some of you to-
night and say, "How do you think people get
eternal life?" some of you would answer something
like this, "If a man leads a very good life, and
fights against sin, and overcomes it, and is faithful in his service to God, at the end of a life of
struggling and victory and service perhaps God will
give him eternal life." Thank God that is not the
doctrine of that Book. The doctrine of that Book
is, that when God sent His Son Jesus Christ down
to this world, He sent eternal life in Him, and the
moment you take Christ you have the eternal life
that is in Him; and if the worst outcast in London
should here and now take Christ, the moment he
did it he would have eternal life.

II. WHAT WE MUST DO WITH JESUS CHRIST

Now, I want to call your attention to a second line
of thought, and that is, What we must do with Jesus
Christ; and let me say at the outset that every

one of us will have to do something with Jesus
Christ to-night. You don't want to. Many a man
here to-night does not want to do anything with
Jesus Christ. You do not want to accept Him or
reject Him. You do not want to confess Him or
deny Him. You just want to get Him off your
hands. You can't do it! Pontius Pilate, who
asked the question of our text, tried to get Christ
off his hands; first he turned to the Jews and said,
" Judge Him according to your law ; " but they said,
" We cannot do it; by our law He ought to die,
but we have not the power to put Him to death."
Pilate then sent Him to Herod, and said, " You take
Him and judge Him," and then Pilate said to himself, " I have got rid of Him now ; I have put the
responsibility on Herod." But look, what is that
coming down the street ? They are the returning
soldiers of Herod, and Herod has sent Christ back
to Pilate; so Pilate has Him on his hands again.
Then Pilate says, " What shall I do ? I do not
want to crucify this Man, because I know He is
innocent, and I do not want to release Him, because
it will make the Jews angry. I know what I will
do," and he went to face that great Jewish mob, and
said to them, " This is the time of Passover, and
you know we have a custom at this time of the
year that there should be released to you one of
the criminals in custody, whosoever you may choose.
Now I am disposed to be gracious to-day, and I will
let you have whom you like ; which will you have,
Jesus or " (and he put up against Jesus the meanest
criminal he had, a murderer and a robber, and he
said to himself, they will never choose him, in the

world) " will you have Jesus or Barabbas ? " But the
men of Jerusalem were like you men of London,
and they cried, " We will have Barabbas ; " and
Pilate had Jesus on his hands again. He could
not get Him off his hands—neither can you.
Every man and every woman in this building
will do something with Jesus Christ to-night. Now
let me tell you what you must do.

1. *You must either accept Him or reject Him.*
Jesus Christ is here, and now offers Himself to
every man and every woman in this building as
your Saviour and Lord and Master, and unless you
definitely accept Him as such you definitely reject
Him. Every man and woman will go out of this
building to-night either having definitely accepted
Christ or definitely rejected Him.

I said to a gentleman going out of a meeting like
this one night, " Mr. ——, are you going to accept
Christ to-night ? " He replied, " I am not going to
accept Him to-night, but I want you to understand
that I do not reject Him." I said, " I understand
nothing of the kind ; Jesus Christ offers Himself to
you, and if you do not accept Him, your refusal to
accept Him is to reject Him ; and every man and
woman in Mildmay Hall will go out of the building
to-night either having accepted Jesus Christ or
having rejected Jesus Christ.

2. Secondly, *we must either confess Him or deny
Him.* He Himself said so in Matthew x. 32, 33 :
" Whosoever therefore shall confess Me before men,
him will I confess also before My Father which is
in Heaven ; but whosoever shall deny Me before
men, him will I also deny before My Father which

is in Heaven." You will do one or the other.
There are just two parties in the world to-day, the
confessed followers of Christ and the deniers of
Christ, and you belong to one or the other.   Which
do you belong to ?   Are you a confessor of the Son
of God, or are you a denier of the Son of God ?

3. In the third place, *you must either let Him
into your heart or shut Him out.* The Lord Jesus
Christ says in Revelation iii. 20 : " Behold I stand at
the door and knock ; if any man hear My voice and
open the door, I will come in to him and will sup
with him, and he with Me."   The Lord Jesus is in
Mildmay Hall to-night, knocking, knocking !   Who
is it knocking ?   The Son of God—knocking at
your heart and mine.   Will you throw your heart
wide open and say, " Come in, Lord Jesus ? " or will
you shut your heart and bar it and say, " Stay out,
Lord Jesus ? "   Every one of us will say one or the
other to-night.

4. In the next place *we must either be for Christ
or against Him.* He Himself says so.   In Matthew xii. 30, he says, " He that is not with Me is
against Me."   Every man that is not with Him is
against Him.   Every man that is not openly,
decidedly, confessedly, out and out, for Christ is
against Christ.   You either have to take your
stand with John, the beloved Apostle, and Peter
the warm-hearted, and Paul the heroic, and all the
noble band of confessors and martyrs and servants
of the Son of God, or you have to take your stand
with Pontius Pilate, with Herod, with Annas and
Caiaphas, with Judas Iscariot.   Where do you take
your stand to-night ?   I could run a line through

this building, and, if I knew you all to-night as God knows you, I could put every man and woman in the building on one or the other side of the line. On one side those who are for Christ, whole-heartedly for Christ ; on the other side those who are against Christ.   Suppose I did it ; which side would you be on ?

III. Who this Jesus is with Whom we have to do

Now one other line of thought, and that is who this Jesus is with whom we have to do.   Who is He ?

1. In the first place, *He is One whom God hath appointed and anointed to be your King*.   We read in Acts ii. 36, " This same Jesus, whom ye have crucified, God hath made both Lord and Christ " (that means " anointed King ").   You have a way of saying here in England that King Edward is your divinely appointed king, and I believe it.   I believe he is, but in an infinitely higher sense Jesus of Nazareth is your divinely appointed and divinely anointed King.   If you reject Jesus Christ, you reject your divinely appointed King ; if you deny Jesus Christ, you deny your divinely appointed King ; if you shut Jesus Christ out of your heart, you shut your divinely appointed King out of your heart ; and if you take your stand against Jesus Christ, you take your stand against your divinely appointed King.   And you are guilty of—listen—*high treason !*   There closed a trial in London the day before yesterday in which a man was tried and convicted of high treason, and sentenced to death.   Whether or not

they will carry out the sentence into execution I do not know; but I do know that if the man was guilty, as the jury found, then according to the English law, and the law of any well-organised government, he is worthy of death. But, men and women, I charge every man and woman in this building to-night—I care not what position in society you hold —I charge you, I indict you, every man and woman, every man and woman in the building out of Christ, of high treason against Heaven's King, and if you got your just deserts, you would die.

One day in Maryborough, over in Australia, a fine-looking man came to see me, an unusually fine-looking man, with splendid physique and dome-like forehead. He said, " I want a talk with you; " and I said, " Very well, take a seat, sir." He said, " I don't know about your preaching. Now I am a moral, upright man, and no one can deny it. Now," he said, " I would like you to tell me what you have got against me." I said, " Are you a Christian ? " " No, sir," he replied. " Have you taken Jesus Christ as your personal Saviour, and surrendered your life to Him as your Lord and Master, and confessed Him as such before the world, and given your life to Him ? " " No, sir," he replied. " Then," I said, " I charge you, sir, with high treason against your King. Jesus Christ is your King; God made Him so; and I charge you, sir "—and I looked him right in the eye—" I charge you, sir, with the crime of high treason against your King." And a dark cloud came over the man's face as he got up, and, going out of my room, he said, " Good afternoon," and walked away.

Months passed away; we had been over to Tasmania and conducted a mission there, and had returned, and I was preaching in Ballarat, about forty miles away from Maryborough. After the service, a fine-looking man came to me, and said, " Do you remember me ? " I knew his face, but I could not remember where I had seen him. I said, " I have seen you somewhere, but I cannot place you." He said, " Do you remember ever charging a man with high treason ? " I said, " I have charged many a man with high treason." " Yes," he said; " but do you remember charging any specific man with high treason ? " Then he began to tell me his story, and I commenced to gather who he was. He said, " I am the man, and I have come to Ballarat, sir, to tell you that you will never charge me with high treason again; " and he held out his hand, and I held out mine, and he took mine in his mighty grip—and it was a mighty grip !—and he said " Down ! " and he dropped on his knees, and I dropped on to mine, and he said, " Lord Jesus, I hand in my allegiance; I give up my treason; I take Thee as my King."

You men ought to do it to-night. He is your King, and every man and woman among you that does not accept Him and acknowledge Him as such to-night I charge you with high treason against Heaven's King.

2. But he is more than your King—*He is the Son of God.* He is a divine Person, and if you reject Him you are guilty of rejecting the Son of God; if you deny Him you are guilty of denying the Son of God; if you shut Him out of your hearts

you are guilty of shutting the Son of God out of
your hearts; if you take your stand against Him
you are guilty of taking your stand against the Son
of God.

"Oh, but," some may say, "we don't believe He
is the Son of God.   Don't you know there are
some people in these advanced days that don't
believe that Jesus is the Son of God?"   I know it
just as well as you do; and I know something else
that you will know in a minute—that is, that denying a fact does not alter the fact.   In this superficial
twentieth century we have a very easy way of dis-
posing of the facts we don't like to believe.   We
say, "I don't believe this," and we think that does
away with the fact.   Men who do not want to
believe in hell say, "I don't believe in hell," and
they think that they have shut the gates of hell
by saying that.   Men who don't want to believe
in the Bible say, "I don't believe in the Bible,"
and they think that they annihilate the Book that
has stood for nineteen centuries by saying that.
Men who do not want to believe in Christ say,
"I do not believe that Jesus Christ is the Son of
God," and they think by their not believing it He
ceases to be the Son of God.   Has it never occurred
to you that a fact is a fact whether you believe it
or not ?   We have got some people in America that
have become so possessed with the idea that denying a thing is quite sufficient to annihilate it, that
they declare that there is no such thing as pain.
They tell you not to believe there is such a thing
as pain, and then you won't feel it.   But when they
go to the dentist's and get into the chair they jump

just as much as any one else! And in this foolish
belief they are dying by the score; by the miserable
madness of Christian Science, that dares to deny
sickness, which exists all the same, and sweeps them
into premature graves. Denying a fact does not
alter a fact, and denying that Jesus is the Son of
God does not alter the fact that He is the Son of
God. It only makes you guilty of robbing a divine
Person of the honour that is His due. Listen:
there are five indisputably divine testimonies to
the deity of Jesus Christ. In the first place, there
is the testimony of the divine life He lived, for
He lived as never man lived. Napoleon Buonaparte
said, " I know men, but Jesus Christ was no (mere)
man." In the second place, there is the testimony
of the divine words He spoke, for He spoke as never
man spoke. In the third place, there is the testimony of the divine works He wrought, for He wrought
as never man wrought; not merely healing the sick,
but cleansing the lepers, stilling the tempest, raising
the dead, and feeding the five thousand by a creative
act with five small loaves and two small fishes. In
the fourth place, then, is the divine attestation of
the resurrection from the dead. The resurrection
of Christ from the dead is the best proven fact of
history; it is proved by such indisputable evidence
that I wish I had time to do in London what I did
in Sydney, meet the sceptics and agnostics of the
city, and prove to them that Jesus rose from the
dead; and I believe I should see in some of your
agnostics and sceptics the honesty which some of
the Sydney sceptics showed, in owning their argu-
ments beaten and coming right out and acknow-

ledging the truth of the resurrection of Jesus Christ. Jesus did rise from the dead. Before they crucified Him He said, " You will crucify Me, but God will set His seal on My claims by raising Me from the dead." They did not believe Him; the Unitarians of the day crucified Him for claiming to be the Son of God. They laid Him in a sepulchre, and put the seal of the Roman Government on the stone, which no one dared to break. But on the third day the Spirit of the living God breathed through the sleeping clay, and the crucified Christ rose from the dead, and God proclaimed in unmistakable tones to all ages, " This is My beloved Son." In the fifth place, there is the testimony of His divine influence upon all subsequent history. There is no question that Jesus Christ claimed to be divine; no competent student will deny that He claimed to be divine. Well, then, He was one of three things; He was either divine, as He claimed to be, or else He was the most audacious impostor the world has ever seen, or else He was the most hopeless lunatic the world has ever seen. He must have been one of these three. Of all the irrational systems of philosophy that of Unitarianism is the most irrational. It says that Jesus Christ was not divine, but was a good man, perhaps the best man that ever walked the earth. I say if He was not divine He was not good, for He was an impostor. You had a man in this city a few months ago who claimed to be divine, and you all decided that he was either an impostor, or most of you, perhaps, took the more charitable view that he was a lunatic. Jesus Christ was either divine, as He claimed to be,

or else He was the most audacious impostor the
world has ever seen, or else He was the greatest
lunatic. Take your choice. Is there any man here
to-night that will say that Jesus Christ was a
lunatic, and that His influence on history has been
the influence of a lunatic? Nobody but a lunatic
will say so. Will any man here dare to say that
the influence of Jesus Christ on the history of the
world has been the influence of an impostor? No
one but an impostor would say so. Then if not a
lunatic or an impostor, what? The Son of God!
Jesus Christ is the Son of God, and every man or
woman that goes away from here to-night rejecting
Christ will go away rejecting the Son of God.
Every man or woman that goes away from here
to-night denying Christ will go away denying the
Son of God. Every man or woman that goes away
from here to-night shutting Christ out of his heart
will go away shutting the Son of God out of his
heart. Every man or woman that goes away from
here to-night taking his stand against Christ will go
away taking his stand against the Son of God. Men,
if you were not blinded by sin to the thought of
your awful guilt, you would fall on your faces now
and cry, "God be merciful to me, so awful a sinner!"
I trust some of you will do it before you go away.

3. *Jesus Christ is not* only your King; He is not
only divine; He is something more yet. You say,
What? *Your Saviour, the One who was wounded
for your transgressions, bruised for your iniquities,
upon whom the chastisement of your peace was laid;*
and oh, men and women, if you reject Him, if you
deny Him, if you take your stand against Him,

if you shut Him out of your hearts, you will be guilty of the most awful ingratitude. Never mother loved her son, never mother suffered for her child, as Christ has loved us and suffered for us. "Though He was rich, yet for our sakes He became poor, that we through His poverty might become rich. Being in the form of God, He thought it not a thing to be grasped to be equal with God, but He emptied Himself and took upon Himself the form of a servant, and was made in the likeness of man, and became obedient unto death, yea, the death of the Cross." For you and me! Will you, will you reject Him, will you deny Him, will you shut Him out of your hearts, and will you take your stand against Him? Oh, men and women, what are you made of?

A man came to me one night and said: "I don't believe in your Christianity." I said, "Why not?" He said, "It is irrational." I asked why. "Why," he said, "you teach, don't you, that if a man leads a moral life and does his duty by his neighbour and in business, treating his employees fairly, he will be lost for ever for nothing worse than the one thing of rejecting Jesus Christ. That is not just," he said. I said, "Hold on a minute; suppose you have a mother who is one of the purest women who ever lived. Suppose your mother loved you even as few mothers loved their sons. Suppose your mother if necessary was ready to lay down her life for you to save yours." He said, "She would." "Suppose you should do your duty," I said, "by your wife and children and by your neighbour, and in your place of business, and treat everybody honestly; suppose

you were upright in all the relations of life, and
treated every person right but one, and that one
your mother, who, you say, is so good, who, you
say, would be ready to die for you, who, you say,
loves you so.   Suppose you should turn her out of
doors on to the street, leaving her there naked and
to starve.   What would you think of yourself ? "
He said, " I would be a scoundrel."   " Well," I
said, " Jesus Christ loves you more than a mother
ever did, and Jesus Christ would not only die for
you, but He did die for you.   Jesus Christ has
done more for you than any mother ever did for
her child.   And now, while you say you are doing
your duty by everybody else, you are trampling
under foot Jesus Christ."   I said, " What do you
think of yourself ? "   He saw it, that he was a
scoundrel.   And he was.   And so are you, and so
are you, every one of you, that is rejecting Jesus
Christ.   Supposing you had a man here in London
who did his duty to his wife and children, who did
his duty by his neighbour, who did his duty in
politics, in business, and by every person but one,
and that one his mother who loved him and
brought him up, who had wasted her life upon him,
and was now feeble and decrepit simply because she
poured her life out for him.   And while he did his
duty by everybody else, he turned that mother, to
whom he owed everything, out into the street to
starve.   Would his doing his duty towards his
wife cover the infamy of his treatment to his
mother ?   Would his doing his duty towards his
neighbour cover the infamy of that treatment ;
would the doing of his duty in politics, in business,

cover the infamy of his treatment of his mother?
Never! And will your doing your duty by your
wife, mother, father, children, brothers, sisters, and
neighbours, cover the infamy, the hideous black
ingratitude of your treatment of the Christ who
gave up Heaven and died on the Cross for you?
Never! You are rejecting the one that was
wounded for your transgressions, bruised for your
iniquities, upon whom the chastisement of your
peace was laid; you are denying every day of your
lives the One who was wounded for your transgressions, bruised for your iniquities, upon whom the
chastisement of your peace was laid; you are shutting out of your heart the One who was wounded
for your transgressions, bruised for your iniquities,
upon whom the chastisement of your peace was laid;
you are taking your stand against the One who was
wounded for your transgressions, bruised for your
iniquities, upon whom the chastisement of your
peace was laid.

Oh, men and women of London, in the light of
what depends on your choice, in the light of what
Jesus Christ is, what are you going to do with Christ
to-night?

It was an awful crisis in the life of Pontius Pilate
when he asked the question of the text. There sat
Pontius Pilate in all the dignity and power of a
Roman governor; and there stood Jesus Christ in
all the beauty of His perfect manhood, in all the
dignity and glory of His perfect Deity, in all the
wondrousness of His matchless love; and there sat
Pontius Pilate deep in thought, deciding what to do.
There were two kinds of voices speaking in Pilate's

heart—higher voices and lower voices; heavenly voices and infernal voices. Listen to the higher voices. The voice of reason said, "Pilate, release Him; He is innocent." The voice of conscience said, "Pilate release Him; He is innocent." The voice of the Spirit of God, whispering in Pilate's heart, said, "Pilate, release Him." The voice of common decency said, "Pilate, release Him; He is innocent." Everything that was noble and true and just in Pilate's heart said, "Release Him." But, alas, there were other voices, infernal voices, speaking, and Pilate is listening to them. There was the voice of cowardice, of fear of what the Jews will say, that whispered, "Pilate, crucify Him." There was the voice of avarice, the greed for gold, saying, "Pilate, crucify Him." There was the voice of low political policy whispering, "Pilate, crucify Him." And Pilate sits there deep in thought. At last, he decides, and he decides wrong; and his name has come down to everlasting infamy.

It is a more solemn moment and a more awful crisis for you to-night, for you know better who Jesus is. There you sit, and there stands Jesus again, unseen, but there He surely stands, in all the dignity and beauty of His perfect manhood; there He stands in all the glory of His perfect Deity; there He stands in all the wondrousness of His matchless love, crowned with thorns, and with pierced hands. And there you sit, trying to decide what to do with Him. In your heart there are higher voices and lower voices. There is the voice of the Spirit of God which says, "Accept Him; confess Him; take your stand on His side to-night."

N

There is the voice of conscience which says, " Accept Him." There is the voice of gratitude which says, " Accept Him." Everything that is noble and good and true in you says, " Accept Him ; confess Him ; let Him into your heart ; take your stand on His side." But, alas, there are lower voices in your heart to-night. There is in your heart the voice of cowardice, the fear of what people will say, which says, " Reject Him to-night ; take your stand against Him." There is the voice of avarice, the greed for gold that might slip through your fingers if you became a real Christian, and that says, " Reject Him." There is the voice of lust, low and beastly, that says, " Reject Him." There is the voice of low political trickery, which says it will rob you of influence in your political party if you become a Christian, and that says, " Reject Him." Everything that is low and base and mean and devilish in your heart says, " Reject Him ; deny Him ; shut Him out of your heart ; take your stand against Him."

Men and women, which are you going to listen to ? what are you going to decide ? God help you to decide right to-night.

XIII

ONE OF THE SADDEST UTTERANCES THAT EVER FELL FROM THE LIPS OF THE SON OF GOD

" Ye will not come to Me, that ye might have life."—JOHN v. 40.

THAT is one of the saddest utterances that our Saviour ever spoke. I wish I could reproduce His tender tones and His loving look when He uttered the words. I believe it would break your heart. He came down from Heaven with its glory to earth with its shame, to bring life to men. He went up and down among men proclaiming that life could be obtained by simply coming to Him, but men would not come. And at last He turned round upon the men who had not come to Him, and with a heart aching with disappointment, and with tones full of yearning pity He said: " Ye will not come to Me, that ye might have life."

I. WHY ANY MAN IS LOST

Those words contain the explanation why any man is lost. If any man is lost it will be because he will not come to Christ. If any man or woman goes out of this hall to-night unsaved, that will be the reason. Jesus Christ offers life to every man and woman here on the simple condition that you come to Him, and if you go out of this hall to-night without it, it is simply because you would not come to Him.

1. No man is lost because he needs to be lost. No man needs to be lost. God has provided salvation for everybody. The atonement of Jesus Christ covers the sins of every man. He tasted death—as we are told in the Word of God—for every man, and the offer of salvation is made to every man. If any man does not take it, it is because he will not come and get it. No man is lost because of any purpose or decree of God. It is the will of God, we are told expressly in His word, that all men should be saved, and He " is not willing "—as we read in 2 Peter iii. 9—" that any should perish, but that all should come to repentance." And if any man is lost, it is solely because He will not come.

2. No man is lost because he has gone down so deeply into sin. Indeed it is true that all of us have gone down into sin so deeply that we deserve to be lost. But " this is a faithful saying, and worthy of all acceptation, that Christ Jesus came into the world to save sinners "—even the chief. He can do it. He is doing it every day. Christ did save the chief of sinners—Saul of Tarsus—and He has power to-night to save any man or woman in London. No man or woman is lost because they have gone down so deeply into sin, but simply because they will not come to that only Saviour who has power to save them from their sins.

3. No man is lost because he is too weak to lead the Christian life. It is true that every one of us

is too weak to lead a true Christian life in our own
strength; but, thank God, we have a Saviour who
"is able to keep us from falling, and to present us
faultless before the presence of His glory with exceeding joy." If any man is lost, it is solely because
he will not come to Christ. If any man or woman
or young person goes out of this hall to-night unsaved it is no one's fault but your own, and the
whole reason will be that you will not come to
Christ and obtain life.

II. WHY MEN WILL NOT COME TO CHRIST

But why will not men come to Christ? There
are many things that keep them from coming.

1. The first one is *sin*. I believe that sin is
keeping more men and women from coming to
Christ than almost anything else. There are a
great many men in this world who know their
need of a Saviour, who long for a Saviour, who have
a deep desire to take the Lord Jesus Christ, but
they know if they come to Him they must leave their
sins behind. A man cannot come to Christ and
retain his sin. You have to choose between Jesus
Christ and sin. Men know that, but they are not
willing to give up their sins. At one of Mr. Moody's
services in Chicago, after he had preached on the
"Prodigal Son," a fine-looking young fellow came to
me and said, "That was a good sermon to-night.
He pictured my case exactly. I am that prodigal
son." I said, "Don't you want to come home to
the Father to-night, then?" He said, "I do." I
said, "And the Father wants you to come." He

said, "I know it." I said, "Will you come?" He
said, "I will not." I asked, "Why not?" He replied, "I am entangled in the meshes of a disgusting
sin." "Then," I said, "will you not give it up to-
night?" "No, sir," he said, "I will not." That
young man went out of that place where he had
been brought face to face with God's love, deliberately choosing a vile sin and death instead
of Jesus Christ and eternal life. I daresay there
are men and women who will go out of this hall
to-night with a clear view of the fact that they can
come to Christ and be pardoned, but you will not
come because there is some definite sin in your life
or heart that you are not willing to give up.

2. *The love of money keeps many men from coming
to Christ.* Many a man knows that if he came
to Christ he would lose money by it. There
are things in his business that would need to be
given up. But he is not willing to sacrifice the
profits he gets in crooked ways. He is deliberately
choosing a larger income and eternal death instead
of Jesus Christ and eternal life. How many a young
fellow has come to me and when I have urged him to
come to Christ he has said, "I believe it is a good
thing, but I should have to give up my situation if
I did." Two young ladies said to Mrs. Torrey at one
of our services in Australia, when they seemed to be
very near decision, "We cannot come to Christ. We
are employed in a large shop, and our employer requires us to misrepresent the goods. We cannot do
that and be Christians, can we?" "No, you cannot,"
Mrs. Torrey replied; and the young ladies said, "If
we don't, then we lose our positions." God pity the

man or the merchant who requires his employees to lie! And yet there are such who profess to be Christians. God have mercy on such hypocrites, who are hurrying on fast to an eternal hell—every one of them. How sad it is that those young women were ready to choose their position and small salary in the place of Jesus Christ and life eternal!

3. *Love of pleasure is keeping many a man and woman from coming to Christ.* How many young men and young women there are in London who know they need Christ and would like to be Christians, but they say if they come to Christ they will have to give up this or that pleasure—the dance or the card party or the theatre. "I can never do it," they say, and they are choosing the dance or card party or theatre or some other form of worldly amusement and death instead of Jesus Christ and life. Dr. John Hall, of New York City, was at one time pastor of perhaps the wealthiest church in New York City. There came to him one day a young lady who was a most beautiful waltzer, and she said, "If I become a Christian will I have to give up my dancing?" He replied, "If you become a Christian and Jesus Christ asks you to give up your dancing, you must be ready to do it." She replied, "If I must choose between Jesus Christ and dancing, I will hold on to my dancing and let Jesus Christ go." What an awful choice! You have not said it; perhaps you never thought it so definitely; but some of you to-night are making that very choice. You feel you could not be a real Christian and hold on to your worldly pleasure, and you reject Jesus Christ rather than give up your worldly pleasure. You are saying by

your action, " if I must choose between Jesus Christ and my dancing or card-playing or theatre, or this or that and the other thing, I will hold on to my dancing, or whatever it be, and let Jesus Christ go."

4. *The fear of man* is keeping many a man and woman in London from coming to Christ and obtaining eternal life.   How many there are who when the invitation is given would like to stand up, but they say if I should do it my friends in business or society would hear about it, and what would they say ?   You keep your seat and you reject Jesus Christ for fear of what they would say.   In Proverbs xxix. 25, we read : " The fear of man bringeth a snare."   It is bringing a snare that is landing many in a path that leads to eternal ruin instead of to Jesus Christ and life eternal.   I would a great deal rather that men would laugh at me down here for doing a wise thing, than that the devils in hell should laugh at me for all eternity for doing a foolish thing.   We have in our country a very foolish custom.   I think you have it to a certain extent in your country also, but perhaps not to the same extent as we have it in ours.   It is called " April Fools' Day."   On the first day of April all the fools in America try to make fools of all the other fools.   One custom is to bore a hole in a silver coin, and after attaching a string to it, put it on the sidewalk.   When any one comes along and stoops to pick it up, the coin is pulled away, and they cry "April fool."   Another joke is to take a wallet and fill it with dust and dirt and chips and throw it on the sidewalk, and when any one picks it up and opens it to cry " April fool ! "   One day a

farmer went to his bank in Baltimore and drew some money, which he put for safe keeping into his wallet. After walking some distance, he felt in his pocket and found the wallet had gone. Retracing his steps, he had not gone many blocks when he saw a circle of people round a wallet, no one daring to touch it, thinking it was full of sawdust and shavings. When the farmer entered the circle and picked up the wallet, all cried "April fool!" but when he opened it and counted the money to see if it were all there, they felt that they were the fools. I tell you that a day is coming for those men and women who laugh at you, because you choose Christ and eternal life, when they will say that you have made a wise choice and they were the fools. Don't let them laugh you out of life eternal. At one of my missions I asked a woman how she was getting on. She replied, "I am not getting on at all; I am perfectly miserable." "Why is that?" I said. "I don't know," she replied. Another said, "I can tell you why it is, she has never told her husband she has accepted Jesus Christ." "Is that so?" I asked her. "It is," she replied. "But you stood up in the meeting?" I said. "Yes, but not when he was present." "Well, you must tell him." "I can't tell my husband; he would laugh at me," she answered. "Never mind how much he laughs," I said. "I can't do it," was all she would reply. The next Sunday night the lady and gentleman were sitting together in one of the front seats. I stopped in the midst of my address and said, "Every woman in the house who will say that from this time on my husband shall have an out-and-out Christian

for his wife, please rise." This woman immediately
rose to her feet. "Now," I said, "every man who
will say from this time my wife shall have a true
Christian man for her husband, please rise." That
man was the first man in the house on his feet.
Show people the beauty and power of a living faith
in Jesus Christ, and you will bring them with you.

5. *An unforgiving spirit* is another thing that is
keeping men and women from coming to Jesus
Christ. They know they cannot come, and bring
a heart full of hate, and so they choose bitterness
and hatred and death instead of Christ and life. One
afternoon at Cleveland, after Mr. Moody had been
speaking, he brought me to a lady to show her the
way of life. I had been speaking to her trying
this and that passage to see what was in the way
of her accepting Christ, when suddenly I turned to
her and said, "Is there somebody you cannot forgive?" She looked quickly at me, and said, "Who
told you?" I said, "Nobody told me, and I have
never seen you before to-night." That was her
trouble, and that is the trouble with some of you.
Some one has done you an injury, or you think they
have, and you will not come to Jesus Christ because you want to cherish this bitter grudge in
your heart. I once talked about two hours to a
young lady, trying to lead her to Christ, but at
last she said, "There is somebody I cannot forgive." I told her, "You must, or be lost for ever."
But she replied, "I cannot; they have done me a
wrong," I said, "If they had not done you a wrong,
there would not be anything to forgive. Have they
wronged you as much as you have wronged Jesus

Christ ? " In the eighteenth chapter of Matthew, commencing at the twenty-third verse, we have the parable of the servant who was forgiven a large debt, and then would not forgive his fellow-servant a trifling sum. That is a picture of the unforgiving one to-day. I said to her, " Read that incident; you must forgive." But she said, " I can't." " Are you willing," I then asked her, " that God should take the bitterness out of your heart ? " She replied, " I am." Then I said, " Kneel down and ask Him; " and she knelt down, and scarcely had her knees touched the floor, when she burst into tears, as she felt the feeling of hate taken away. Are you going to reject Jesus Christ and eternal life for the sake of hating somebody ? God have mercy upon you.

6. *Self-will* stands between many a person and Christ and eternal life. There are a great many people in this world who are not willing to surrender their wills to anybody, not even to God. They are bound to have their own way. A woman told me that on Friday night. She said, " I cannot give my will up to anybody." What foolishness ! Who is this God to whom we ask you to surrender your will ? God is love. Is it not wisdom to surrender our wills to infinite love and wisdom ? Oh, the folly of those who will not surrender their wills to God and His love.

7. There is one more thing that is keeping people from coming to Jesus Christ, and that is *pride*. I believe that there are thousands and tens of thousands of people in London to-night that are kept from Him because of the pride of their hearts. Pride

manifests itself in many ways. It makes men and women, who have led moral and respectable lives, unwilling to admit that they are lost sinners, and must come into the kingdom of God through the same door as the thief or the harlot or the drunkard. You will all have to get into the kingdom in that way. Look at Christ's parable of the publican and sinner. First there came the Pharisee to the temple to pray, a moral, upright, prominent citizen. But what is his prayer? It is just a parade of his own virtues. "God, I thank thee, that I am not as the rest of men, extortioners, unjust, adulterers, or even as this publican. I fast twice in the week; I give tithes of all that I possess." Do you know what Jesus Christ says about him? He says that this man went down to his house unforgiven. Then came the publican—an outcast, despised by everybody, but a man who had been brought to the consciousness of his sin. He " would not lift up so much as his eyes unto Heaven, but smote upon his breast, saying, ' God be merciful to me a sinner ' " — *the* sinner. Do you know what Jesus Christ says? " I tell you, this man went down to his house justified rather than the other; for every one that exalteth himself shall be abased; and he that humbleth himself shall be exalted." I believe that very many people are being kept from Christ and eternal life by the pride of their hearts. In Chicago I was once telling the story of a woman who had been away down in sin and been saved; and afterwards a refined lady came to me and said, "You do not mean to say that *that woman* was saved?" The strange thing was that the lady was a Univer-

salist, and believed that everybody could be saved.
I told her "the woman was saved, and what is more,
she was saved in precisely the same way that you will
be saved if you ever are saved." That is God's
truth. Ah! but some of you people are not willing
to lay your pride in the dust. You are not willing
to throw your pride to the winds, and go to God
and seek pardon through the atoning blood of the
Son of God. You will never be saved any other
way. A lady once came to me and said, " My
Christian experience is not satisfactory." I said,
" I don't think you have any Christian experience."
"Why," she said, "I have. I am the widow of a minister
and a member of a church." " Well," I responded,
" I don't think that you were ever saved in your
life. No, you never were, for you never saw yourself as a lost sinner in your life." She said, " I
never did, because I am not." I replied, " Let me
deal frankly with you. You are just full of conceit.
Unless God opens your eyes to see that you are not
essentially better than the vilest sinner, and unless
you come to God and cry for mercy through the
atoning blood of Christ, you will never be saved."
She said, " You are cruel." " No," I said, " I am
kind. You are a physician, I believe?" She
replied, "Yes." Then I said, " Suppose a patient
had a tumour, and you cut it out to save her life.
Would you call that cruel?" " No," she said, " I
should say that was the kindest thing I could do."
" Well," I said, " you have a tumour. Your pride
and conceit are blinding your eyes so that you
cannot see that you are a poor, vile, worthless sinner,
and Jesus Christ died for you on the Cross." The

woman had the good sense at last to see it, but that is more than some of you have. I tell you among the people who are in this hall there are a lot of people who are being kept away from Christ by spiritual pride.

But pride operates in another way. Oh, that by the help of God I could tear these awful scales from your eyes. Pride makes people set themselves not to do certain things which they are asked to do. " I am not coming," they say, " to the meeting," or " I am not going to the front seats," or " I am not going to the inquiry room. A person can be saved without that." They can, beyond a doubt ; but if you make it a point that you won't do something of that kind, you won't be saved until you do. In Mr. Finney's day many people found salvation under a certain tree. One prominent man said he would not go out there. It was not necessary, of course. He did all sorts of things, but he would not do that. He got no peace, however, and one day he stole out of the town the back way, and made his way to the place where the tree was, and climbed the fence around it. When he went to kneel down the wind shook a leaf and frightened him. But as soon as he knelt down and asked God, He saved him right there. There are some of you men and women like that. Do not misunderstand me. I want to make it as clear as day. It is not necessary for you to do anything except to believe in the Lord Jesus Christ, but if you say I won't do a thing, you will never be saved until you do. You have got to lay your pride in the dust before you can find Jesus Christ. I remember the first time I went to hold a mission.

The last meeting had come, and the last person had stood up, and I got up to dismiss the meeting, when a lady rose. She was the leading society woman in the town. She rose slowly to her feet and said, "Before you dismiss this meeting, may I say something?" And then, turning round to face the audience, she said, "When Mr. Torrey came, I said he would never get me to stand up, but I now wish to most humbly take it all back, and ask you to pray for me." The power of God fell on that meeting. Some of you men and women think your position in society is too exalted for you to come up to the front with common folks and accept the Saviour just as ordinary men and women do, but if you think that, you will never be saved until you humble your pride in the dust, and are willing to go anywhere to find peace and pardon. Let us throw away everything that stands between us and Jesus Christ. He stands in this building to-night with outstretched hands. Oh, see Him! Hear the tender tones that fall from His lips, the heart-breaking tones: "Ye will not come to Me, that ye might have life." The Lord Jesus Christ, who died on the Cross of Calvary, is standing here, with His thorn-crowned brow and pierced hands, saying, "Ye will not come to Me that ye might have life." Men and women, rise and say, "I will come, Lord Jesus; I come now."

XIV

" WHAT ARE YOU WAITING FOR ? "

"And now why tarriest thou? Arise and be baptized, washing away thy sin, calling on the name of the Lord" (especially
the first part of the verse, "Why tarriest thou?").—Acts
xxii. 16.

IT was God who asked the question, through His
servant Ananias, of Saul of Tarsus; and I believe
that God is asking that same question to-night
through me of every man and woman and child
in this building that is not an openly confessed,
out-and-out follower of Jesus Christ. God is saying to you to-night, "Why tarriest thou? What
are you waiting for? Why do you not come out
to-night on the side of Jesus Christ?" You remember that Saul of Tarsus hated Jesus Christ.
Saul of Tarsus thought that Jesus of Nazareth was
an impostor; he did not believe that He was the
Christ and the Son of God as He claimed to be.
But away down in the depths of his heart Saul of
Tarsus had an uneasy feeling that perhaps He was
the Christ, perhaps He was the Son of God, but
he never admitted it even to himself. As far as
his admitted convictions were concerned, Saul of
Tarsus thought Jesus was an impostor, and he
hated Jesus with a very intense hatred; and he
said, "I am going to stamp out this religion of the

followers of Jesus." And he not only hated Jesus Christ, but he hated everybody that bore the name of Christ, and whenever he saw a man or woman or child that believed in Jesus and followed Him, he hated them. He did everything in his power to stamp out the religion of Jesus. He went from house to house in Jerusalem, and arrested men and women and children, sparing neither age nor sex, and dragged them before the courts to be tried; and when they were sentenced to death, he gave his vote for their execution. But at last Saul of Tarsus had exhausted all the opportunities for murder in Jerusalem, but he had not exhausted the hatred of his heart. He breathed an atmosphere of murder and slaughter, and hearing that a hundred and more miles away, in the city of Damascus, there were followers of Jesus, he went, with a heart full of hatred, to the High Priest, and said, "Give me letters to Damascus, and I will go and do in Damascus what I have done in Jerusalem. I will arrest all the Christians, whether men or women or children, and I will bring them down here to Jerusalem to be punished." His request was quickly granted.

It was a long journey across the barren, desolate, dreary desert, whether on foot or on horseback, but day after day Saul of Tarsus presses on, not even staying for the burning heat of the noonday sun. At last he has almost reached Damascus, and he stands on the last hilltop, and there Damascus lies before him in all its beauty, a city of olive groves, a city of vineyards, a city of gardens, and of flashing fountains, a city of glittering palaces and dashing rivers, a city of which poets loved to sing, and of which

o

one Persian poet says, " Damascus is a diamond in
a setting of emeralds."   But as Saul looks down
on Damascus in all its far-famed beauty, he has
no eye for its beauty; his only thought is that in
that city are some of these accursed Christians, and
he adds to himself as he stands there, " I will soon
have them in my power, and be dragging them
back to be punished at Jerusalem."   He starts to
press on towards the city, to do the hellish work
for which he has come, when suddenly there shines
round about him a marvellous light with a brightness
above that of the noonday sun, and there in the
midst of it he beholds the most wondrous face and
form his eyes had ever gazed upon, the face and
form of the glorified Christ.   He is blinded by the
glory of it, and falls on his face to the ground.
He hears a voice speaking to him, " Saul, Saul, why
persecutest thou Me ? " and the humbled man cries
back from the ground, " Who art Thou, Lord ? "
and back comes the crushing and overwhelming
answer, " I am Jesus whom thou persecutest."
Then, thoroughly subdued and awed, he cries back,
" What wilt Thou have me to do, Lord ? "   And the
answer comes, " Arise, stand upon thy feet, and go
into Damascus, and there it shall be told you what
thou must do."   He rises to his feet, but everything
is black.   He turns his eyes hither and thither, but
he sees nothing.   He has to hold out his hand and
be led like a helpless child into the city he ex-
pected to enter as a conqueror.   He goes to the
house of Judas, and there for three days and three
nights he shuts himself up and sees no one, neither
eating, sleeping, nor drinking ; but still he does not
yield himself to Christ.   At last, God, weary of

waiting, sends His servant Ananias with the message,
" Why do you not come out openly and confess
Him whom you know to be the Christ ? "

Men and women, God is putting the same question to you: " Why tarriest thou ? Why do you
not come out openly and accept Christ, and confess
Him before the world as your Saviour and Lord
and Master ? " I wish it were possible for me to
go down from this platform, and to go from seat
to seat, and from man to man, and put to every
man and woman out of Christ this question : What
are you waiting for before you come out on the
side of Christ ? I would have you tell me your
real reason. I would have you give me an honest
answer, and then I would sit down beside you with
the Word of God, and show you how little there
is in your reason. If I could do that I believe
I could get almost every man and woman in this
building that is out of Christ to accept Him to-night.
But there is no time of course for that, it would take
days and weeks and months, so I am going to ask
you to do the next best thing. I am going to ask
every man and woman who is not a Christian to
forget about every one else, and not to look at me
as preaching a sermon to a multitude, but to think
of you and me as being here alone in personal conversation together, face to face. Will you put to
yourself this question before we begin our conversation, " What am I waiting for ? why do I not
come out on the side of Christ to-night ? " Now
we are going to have a few moments of silence
and prayer, and I am going to ask every Christian man and woman in the room to pray that
every one may be honest, and I am going to ask

all of you who are not Christians to put this
question to yourselves, "What am I waiting for?"
Let us have silence.

Will every man and woman put to themselves the
question, "What is the real reason that I do not
accept and confess Christ to-night; what am I waiting for?" Now I will take up your answers one by one.

1. Some of you have said to-night, "*I am waiting until I shall be convinced ;* just as soon as I am
convinced that the Bible is the Word of God and
Jesus is the Son of God, I will accept Christ as my
Saviour, and confess Him before the world." Now,
I want to make an offer to every man and woman
who has made that answer. If you will come to
me at the close of this meeting, I will show you the
way to find out that, beyond all peradventure, the
Bible is God's Word, and Jesus Christ is God's Son.
Now, if you are an honest sceptic, you will accept
that offer, and if you do not accept it, never say
again that you are a sceptic. You are a humbug.
Of course, if you are only a trifler I have no time to
waste upon you, but if you are a sincere doubter,
I would rather speak with you than anybody else
in the building, for I have yet to find the first sincere doubter, the first sincere agnostic, the first sincere atheist, the first spiritualist, the first Christian
Scientist, the first Theosophist, who really wanted to
know the truth, that I could not show the way to
find it. All over the world to-night there are men
who used to be agnostics and doubters whom it has
been my privilege to lead to Jesus. If you are an
honest sceptic, you will accept that offer, and if you
do not, at least one good result will come of it—

you will know when you go out of this hall that you
are not an honest sceptic.   I went to a man one
night during my first pastorate; he was standing
away at the end of the hall between the two doors, and
I stepped up to him and said, " Mr B." (I knew him
very well, he was one of the most prominent business men in the place and one of the most highly
esteemed) " why are you not a Christian ? "   " Well,"
he replied, " I don't boast about it, but I don't believe anything."   I said, " Don't you believe there
is a God ? "   And he said, " I have never given up
faith that there is a supreme Being."   " Well," I
said, " if there is a God, you ought to surrender your
will to Him.   Will you do it ?   Will you take your
stand upon the will of God, and follow it wherever
it carries you ? "   He replied, " I try to live now as
near right as I know how " (I believe he did, for
he was one of the most upright men in the community).   But I said, " That is not what I asked;
will you take your stand upon the will of God, and
follow it wherever it carries you ? "   He said, " I
have never put it in quite that way."   I said, " Will
you put it that way to-night ? "   He said, " I will."
Then I said, " One more thing; do you believe
God answers prayer ? "   " No," he said, " I do not."
He said, " I have often lain awake at night thinking
about that, and I have come to the conclusion that
God does not answer prayer."   " Well," I said, " I
know He does, and you can test it to-day.   Pray
this prayer : ' Oh God, show me if Jesus Christ is
Thy Son or not, and if You show me that He is, I
promise to accept Him as my Saviour, and confess
Him before the world.' "   He said, " I will."   That
same week I saw that gentleman come in to the

prayer meeting at the church, a very unusual thing for him to do, and as soon as I threw open the prayer meeting, I saw this man rise to his feet. He said, " Friends, I doubted everything ; I was in a perfect mist ; I did not know what I believed ; I did not know as I believed anything." Then he told us what he had done. He had been honest with himself and with God and with truth, and he had done what he had promised to do. " And now," he said, " my mists have all gone, and I do not know where they have gone." You say, " I doubt that story." Well, try it for yourselves.

Another man in that same community lived across the street from my house, and I went to see him one evening ; the sun was just setting, and I was standing on his front lawn, talking with him, for, though he was an agnostic and I was a Christian minister, we were good friends. Christians ought not to get off somewhere where nobody of an ordinary kind can touch them. The Word says, " Ye are the salt of the earth." You cannot preserve meat by putting meat in one barrel and salt in another. Well, I was standing on this man's lawn ; suddenly he turned to me—the sun had gone down and there followed a peculiar glow in the sky, and I think he felt a strange influence from it—he said to me suddenly, " Mr. Torrey, I am sixty-six years of age, and I have no one to leave my money to " (and he had a good amount to leave) " I cannot take a penny of it with me, and I would give every penny of it, if I could believe as you do." I said, " I can tell you how." He said, " I wish you would." I said, " Let us go in." We stepped into the house, and I asked his wife for a sheet of paper, and I wrote on it something like this: "I believe there is an absolute difference between right and wrong" —I did not say "I believe there is a God;" he did not affirm or deny that, and I began just where he was—"I believe there is an absolute difference between right and wrong, and I hereby take my stand on the right to follow it wherever it carries me. I promise to make an earnest search to find if Jesus Christ is the Son of God; and if I find that Jesus Christ is the Son of God, I promise to accept Him as my Saviour and confess Him before the world." When I had written that I said, "Mr. H., read that." He read it. "Now," I said, "will you sign that?" "Why, anybody ought to be willing to sign that," he replied. "Well, will *you* sign it?" I said. "All you ask me to sign is what my own conscience tells me I ought to do. Anybody ought to be willing to sign that." "Yes," I said, "but will YOU sign it?" And he said again, "Anybody ought to be willing to sign that." "Will YOU sign it?" "I will think about it."

He never signed it, and he died as he had lived, without God and without hope. He went out into the darkness of a Christless eternity, and I ask you, "Whose fault was it?" Away out in the darkness a light had been shown to him, and he confessed that his own conscience told him that he ought to be willing to follow it, and he would not follow it. Will you follow it? You say you are sceptics and agnostics; so I used to be, but I was an honest man, and when a way was pointed out I tried to see where it led, and, thank God, it led out of the barrenness and desolation and darkness of utter nihilism into a clear faith that cannot be shaken,

that that blessed Book is God's Word, and that
the Christ of that Book is the Son of God.

2. Well, some one else may say, "My case is
different. I believe in the Bible just as much as
you do, but *I am waiting till I have enjoyed the
world enough.*" There are a great many people
of that kind in London. Some of them have grown
old and grey in that condition. They make the
mistake of thinking that when they grow tired of the
world, they can turn to Christ without any sacrifice; they think that after a while a man will grow
tired of the world and give it up without an effort.
What a great mistake! The longer you live for
the world the less enjoyment you get out of it, but
the tighter its grip becomes upon your shrivelling
soul. There will never be another night when it
is so easy to give up the world as it is to-night.
You know that is true in the case of the drinking
man. When a man begins to drink, there is pleasure
in it; the first glass of beer or of wine or of champagne has joy in it, and exhilaration in it—a man
feels like two men; but as a man goes on drinking
there is less and less joy, but the more complete his
slavery becomes, until at last a man reaches a place,
which thousands of men and women in London
have already reached, where they hate alcohol as
much as any prohibitionist, but are utterly unable
to give it up. They know it is robbing them of
their brains, they know it is robbing them of their
manhood, of the respect of the community, of the
affection of their wives, and the confidence of their
children. They know it is taking the bread out of
their children's mouths, and the clothes from their
wives' backs; yet, hating it as they do, they will

take up their glass, filled with liquid damnation, and drink it to the dregs. You say "That is true." It is just as true of the love of money. The slavery of money is as complete and as degrading as the slavery of strong drink. I would rather undertake to save ten drunkards than one money fiend, any day. When a man begins, there is pleasure in it; the first ten pounds, or the first hundred pounds, or perhaps the first thousand pounds that he lays by gives him joy; but as a man goes on accumulating, there is less and less pleasure, and at last there is no pleasure at all, but the man is the slave of the degrading lust for gold. I was visiting a man in the State of Ohio, when I was living in Minneapolis, in the Boom days, when men were making fortunes in a day. The man to whom I refer had a comfortable fortune of about £100,000, and was now upwards of seventy years of age. One foot was in the grave, and the other foot almost over the edge. Only a few weeks before I came to see him, they had to send post-haste for the doctor to come and pull the man's other foot away from the edge of the grave. After everybody else had gone to bed, he said to me in a low tone of voice—what do you think? "Oh," you say, "something about Heaven, something about eternity; a man with one foot in the grave and the other almost over would wish to talk about the future and what it meant for him." But no, he leaned over and said: "Do you know any place up in Minneapolis where I could invest my money where it would bring big interest?" Oh, some of you men are going very fast that same road, selling your souls for damning gold. It is just the same way with the love of pleasure. The first dance, the first card party, the first theatre, oh, the excitement of it and the pleasure of it and the exhilaration of it; but as one goes on the pleasure of these things becomes less and less, and more and more complete does the slavery to them become. The time will never come when you have enjoyed the world enough. Furthermore, there is more joy in Jesus Christ in twenty-four hours than there is in the world in 365 years. I have tried them both.

Further, suppose while you are waiting until you have enjoyed the world enough you are called out of the world. "What shall it profit a man if he gain the whole world and lose his own soul?" One night I went down the aisle almost to the far end of it, and the people were standing up singing, and I turned to a young lady and I said to her, "Why don't you become a Christian?" "Oh," she said, "I enjoy the world too much." I simply quoted God's word to her, "What shall it profit a man if he gain the whole world and lose his own soul?" and passed on. The meetings went on, and the last night came. The last meeting had finished, and, after I had returned to the house where I was staying, my hostess came to me and said, "Two young ladies want to see you; they are waiting in the other room." I went in, and one of them was the young lady of whom I am speaking. I said to her, "Why do you want to see me?" "Oh," she said, "I do not enjoy the world any more; since you spoke to me your words have been ringing in my ears: 'What shall it profit a man if he gain the whole world and lose his own soul?' And I have come to-night, and have brought my friend with me, so that you may tell us what to do to be saved." Oh, that those

words would ring in the ears of some of you men
and women until you cannot rest, until you come to
the Son of God for rest and joy, which is rest and
joy indeed.

3. "*I am waiting for my friend,*" says another.
That is true of a great many persons. Young men
are waiting for their friends, and young ladies are
waiting for their lady friends, women are waiting for
their husbands, lovers are waiting for their sweet-
hearts—one is waiting for another. What I say to
you is, You come to Christ first, and bring your
friends along. If your friends love you as much as
you love them, when you come to Christ they will
come too. It is better that you should take them
to Heaven with you than that they should take you
to hell with them.

I was staying at one time with a minister, and
he told me this story. He said: "After my wife
and I had been married for fourteen and a half years
she turned to me one night and said, 'Husband, I
have made up my mind to be a Christian and to
unite with the Church.'" He said, "I was very
angry; I was the principal of the schools in that
town and held a prominent position, and I said to
her, 'Why, you must not do it; you and I have
lived very happily together for fourteen and a half
years, but if you become a Christian, I have no
intention of becoming one, and that will just separate
us for ever.' But she said to me, 'I must be a
Christian. I love you, and would do almost anything to please you, but I feel I must first please
God.' 'Well,' I said, 'you become a Christian, if
you feel that you want to, but you must not unite
with the Church.' She regarded my wishes in this

respect, and so we went on for six months, she a Christian, and I not. Then she said to me, ' Husband, I must become a member of the Church of Jesus Christ.' " (Of course, if a person is converted they will never be happy out of the Church.) Then her husband said, " I was very angry, and said to her, ' If you do join the Church, I want you to understand that you are nothing more to me. We have lived happily together now for fifteen years, but if you unite yourself with the Church from this time on you go your way, and I shall go mine, and you will be nothing more to me.' She said, ' Husband, I love you, and I would do all I could to please you, but I must first of all please God, and I have made up my mind to unite with the Church to-morrow.' She went to her room, and I went to mine. I was very angry with her. I was getting angrier all the time. I could not sleep. I heard eleven o'clock strike, and I was very angry ; I heard twelve o'clock strike, and I was more angry still; I heard one o'clock, and I was angrier still ; but when two o'clock came, I called out to my wife, ' Wife, I am converted.' " The husband and wife went into the Church together. He became a minister of the Gospel, and to-day he is in Heaven. If that wife had waited for him, they would have gone down to a Christless grave and a Christless eternity together. Oh, men and women, come to Christ and bring your friends with you. Even if they do not come, you come to Christ. I would start for Heaven to-night, even if I had to start, alone. I would rather go to Heaven alone than go to hell in company. I believe that one of the darkest experiences of that dark world

will be when a husband that goes there is met by
the wife whom he dragged there.

In one of my pastorates a solemn thing occurred ;
before I had gone there, in the neighbouring town-
ship there had been a great awakening, and many
people had come out on the side of Christ, and one
night, when the preacher extended an invitation for all
those who would accept Christ to come to the front, a
lady rose from her place to do so. But her husband,
sitting back of her, laid his hand on her shoulder,
and forced her back into her seat. She yielded to
him, and she drifted away from her conviction into
scepticism and blank infidelity. That is the way
people become infidels, by resisting the Spirit of God.
Show me a hundred infidels, and I will show you in
ninety-nine cases men who were under conviction
of sin at some time or other, but who have resisted
the Spirit of God. This lady became an utter atheist.
Some time afterwards there was a revival in the
town. It caused the infidels of the town to be
greatly stirred up. When we get a revival, it stirs
up the infidels wonderfully. They said, " This
cannot go on. We will send off and get one of
our infidel lecturers ; " and they got their lecturer,
a follower of Ingersoll. Thank God, they did have
that lecturer. People went to hear him ; and when
they had heard him, they said, " If that is infidelity,
we do not want any of it." While waiting for this
professor, this lady said, " I can hardly wait for Professor —— to get here." She did not wait. There
was a little card party being held on the Saturday
night, and this lady and her friends were among the
party. Eleven o'clock on Saturday night came, and
they were still playing cards ; at twelve o'clock they

were still playing; and at one o'clock on Sunday morning—on the Lord's Day—they were still playing cards. Sabbath-breaking and card-playing go hand in hand, you know. About one o'clock in the morning this woman sprang to her feet, clapped her hand on her head, and cried, "Oh!" and dropped dead beside the table. I shall never forget my meeting with her husband after that awful day. I had never spoken to him before; but I happened to walk into the post-office, and this man came in at the same time, and he came across the post-office and held out his hand, and, with a grip of despair, he took my hand in his. He knew he had sent his wife into a Christless eternity. Oh, don't wait for others; come yourself, and bring the others with you.

4. "Well," some one else says, "that is not what I am waiting for; *I am waiting for feeling.*" I believe that is true of a great many. There is many an earnest soul that would really like to be a Christian, but they think they have not got the right kind of feeling. Some are *waiting for the joy and peace that Christians talk about.* I went to a young lady once in a meeting like this, and said to her, "Why are you not a Christian?" She replied, "I have not the right kind of feeling. These people have been talking about the joy and peace that they have; I have not any joy like that, and I cannot come to Christ until I get it." I said, "But that is the result of coming. You don't expect the result, do you, before you take the step? Suppose I should go and see a very sick man, and I said to him, "What is the matter with you?" and he said, "Influenza." Then I might say, "I had

the influenza some time ago, and I took such and such a remedy, and it cured me completely." Then he would say, "What is that remedy?" Then, when I tell him what it is, he calls for his man, and tells him to run down to the chemist's at once and buy it; and when he brings the bottle back, the sick man hands it to me and says, "Is that it?" and I say, "Yes, that is the medicine." And he says to me, "You say you took it, and it made you better right off?" and I say, "Yes." Then he says, "Thank you for telling me of it; I am so much obliged." Then a few days afterwards I go to see that man, and expect to find him up and well; but instead of that, I find him still in bed and sicker than ever. I say to him, "I don't understand this. Are you not any better?" "No," he says, "I am worse." "Why, how is that?" I ask; "did you not get that medicine which cured me?" "Yes, of course I got it," he says; "were you not in the room when my man brought it to me from the chemist's?" "Well, did you take it?" I ask. "Oh no, I didn't take it," he says; "you said it made you a great deal better right off. But I did not feel any better, so I did not take it!" You would say, "What a foolish man." Is he any more foolish than you? You cannot expect to have the result of accepting Christ until you take the step; take Christ and confess Him, and you will get all the joy you need.

A woman once came to me in one of our missions and said, "I want to be a Christian." I said, "Become one now." She said, "How?" I said, "It is just as simple as it is to walk home." "Oh, but," she said, "I don't feel any better." I said, "Of

course you don't. You haven't done the thing to
make you feel better." "But all the other folks
talk about their joy," she said. I said, "Yes, because they have taken the step that leads to joy.
Don't you know you are a sinner, and that Christ
died for your sins, and that He is your rightful
Lord and Master?" She said, "Yes, I know that."
"Well," I said, "will you take Him for your Saviour,
and yield to Him as your Lord and Master now?"
She said, "I will." "Then let us get down and pray,"
I said. When we had prayed, I said, "Now it is
too late to confess Christ publicly in the meeting,
for the people have nearly all gone, but you confess
Christ the first chance you get." "But I don't feel
any better," she said. "I did not suppose you
would," I said; "you have not gone far enough yet.
You must confess Christ before the world, and then
the joy and peace will come to you." The next
day, when I went to the town hall, before I went
on to the platform to address the business men's
meeting, I received a note from this lady, which
said: "Oh, Dr. Torrey, I feel so grateful to you; I
am so happy. Fifteen minutes after leaving the
hall last night I had all the joy I could contain.
When I got outside I met my brother, and went
home with him; and on the way I told him that I
had given myself to Christ; and as I told him, the
joy came into my heart, and has been there ever
since."

Other people are *waiting for conviction of sin*.
They feel that they cannot come to Christ, because
they have not shed tears, and are not overwhelmed
with the burden of sin. I like to see conviction of
sin, but there is no passage in the whole Bible that

says you have got to feel sorry before you are saved. In Isaiah lv. 7 we read, "Let the wicked *forsake* his way" (not be sorry about it) "and the unrighteous man his thoughts, and let him return unto the Lord, and He will have mercy upon him; and to our God, for He will abundantly pardon." It doesn't say "feel sorry for your sin;" it says, "quit your sin and turn to God." I have seen people very sorry over their sins; they just weep and weep, and then go right out and do the same thing again for which they have professed to be sorry. I have known people just as stolid as a man could be, but they turned from their sin and took Christ in cold blood, as it were, and God kept His word and saved them. And He will keep His promise to-night.

On one occasion in Chicago I went to preach for a Baptist minister. In the second meeting I sat down by a man and his wife, aged about forty years, and I said to him, "Why are you not a Christian?" He said, "I would like to be; I hope to be a Christian some day. My father was a Baptist minister, and my mother is one of the best women that ever lived on earth." "Well," I said, "come right now." He said, "I want to." I said, "Then why don't you?" He said, "I have not got the right kind of feeling." I said, "What do you think is the right kind of feeling?" He said, "I don't feel sorry for my sins. Don't you think a man ought to have conviction of sin?" I said, "I think you ought, but I do not read in my Bible anything that says a man has to feel sorry to be saved. My Bible says, 'Turn from sin and take Christ'; my Bible says, 'Receive Christ.' 'As many as received Him'—not to as many as wept over

P

their sin—'as many as received Him to them gave
He power to become sons of God.' Don't you know
you are a sinner?" I said. "I know I am a sinner,"
he said, "but I don't feel it." I said, "Don't you
know that Jesus Christ is your Saviour?" "Yes,"
he said. "Don't you know it would be the best
thing you could do to take Him as your Saviour?"
"Yes, I do." Then I said, "Take Him as your
Saviour now." He said, "Without feeling sorry?"
I said, "Never mind the feeling. Will you take
Him?" He said, "I have not any feeling." I said,
"See here, what business are you in?" He said, "I
am in the real estate business." I said, "Suppose
that I should come down to your office to-morrow
morning and offer to sell you a corner lot for five
thousand dollars, and you knew it was a lot that
you could sell in twenty-four hours for ten thousand
dollars, but, for some reason or other, you didn't
feel like buying it—Would you buy it?" He said,
"I would buy it quick, feeling or no feeling." "My
friend," I said, "show the same common-sense in
religion that you do in business. Don't you know
it would be the best paying investment you could
make to take Jesus Christ as your Saviour?" He
said, "Yes, I do." "Will you do it, then, feeling
or no feeling?" He said, "Is that all?" I said,
"That is all to start with." "Then," he said, "I
will do it." I said, "Will you kneel down and seal
the bargain right now?" and we knelt, and he and
his wife took Christ. I went back to that church
in a few months, and that man had come along so
finely that they had made him a trustee of the
church.

Men and women, Christ is a Saviour. God offers

Him to you; you take Him and it is done. Feeling or no feeling, will you take Him to-night?

No one has a good reason for not coming to Christ. There are a thousand reasons why you ought to come. Every year that you have lived has brought you one year nearer to eternity, and is a reason for coming to Christ to-night; every year that you have still to live and that might be a year of service is a reason for coming to Christ to-night. Every saved friend you have is a reason for coming to Christ to-night, that you may spend eternity with him in Heaven. Every unsaved friend that you have is a reason why you should come to Christ to-night, that you may bring him with you. Every thorn in the Saviour's crown, every nail in the Saviour's hands and feet, every stroke laid upon the Saviour's back, when He was wounded for your transgressions and bruised for your iniquities, and the chastisement of your peace was laid upon Him, is a reason for accepting Christ to-night. Will you do it? Oh, there is an awful risk in delay.

A quaint old preacher of the olden days in our country, the Rev. Dan Baker, puts it in the way of a story. He tells of a man who was crossing the ocean. He was leaning over the side of the vessel; it was a bright sunny day, and not a wave broke the surface of the water, just a little ripple here and there kissed by the rays of the sun. And the man, as he leaned over the rail of the vessel, was tossing something in the air, something which, when it fell through the sunlight, sparkled with singular radiance and glory; and he watched it so eagerly as he tossed it up and caught it as it fell. He tossed it up again and again and again, and it threw out its marvellous light as it fell. At last an onlooker came and said, " May I ask what that is that you are tossing up so carelessly ? " He replied, " Certainly ; look at it, it is a diamond." " Is it of much value ? " asked the onlooker. " Yes, of very great value. See the colour of it, see the size of it. In fact, all I have in the world is in that diamond. I am going to a new country to seek my fortune, and I have sold everything I have, and have put it into that diamond, so as to get it into a portable shape." " Then if it is so valuable, is it not an awful risk you are running in tossing it up so carelessly ? " was the next question. " No risk at all. I have been doing this for the last half-hour," said the man. " But there might come a last time," said the onlooker ; but the man laughed and threw it up again, and caught it as it fell, and again and again, and once more, and it flashed and blazed, and looked like a burning coal in the sunlight, and he watches it so eagerly as it falls the last time. Ah, but this time it is too far out. He reaches as far as he can over the rail of the vessel, but he cannot reach far enough. There is a little plash in the ocean. For a moment he stands aghast, and then he cries, " Lost ! lost ! lost ! All I have in the world, lost ! "

You say, " No man would be so great a fool as that ; that story is not true." That story is true, and the man is here to-night. Thou art the man ! That ocean is eternity ; that vessel you are on is life ; that diamond is your soul, of priceless value, that soul that Christ put great enough value upon to die for it, to save it. And you have been trifling with it ! I come to you to-night and say, " My

friend, what is that in your hand which you are
playing with so carelessly?" You say, "It is my
soul." "Is it worth much?" "More than the whole
round earth, 'for what shall it profit a man if he
gain the whole world and lose his own soul?'"
"But don't you think you are taking an awful
risk?" "Oh no," you say, "I have been doing
this for the last five years, for the last ten, fifteen,
or twenty years." "Yes, but you might do it once
too often." "Oh no," you say, and to-night once
more you throw it up. But you may throw it up
once too often; it will fall too far out, beyond
your reach; there will be a plash, and you will try
to look after it; not in the impenetrable depths of
the blue ocean, but in the unfathomable depths of
the bottomless pit it sinks and sinks and sinks, and
you cry, "Lost! lost! lost! my soul is lost!" That
may be your cry some day. Come to-night, before
it is too late, and put your soul where it will be
everlastingly safe, in the keeping of the Son of God.

XV

EXCUSES

"And they all with one consent began to make excuse."—
LUKE xiv. 18.

IN these words our Lord Jesus Christ sets forth the
manner in which God's invitation of love and grace
and mercy would be received, and that is precisely
the way in which God's invitation of mercy is being
received by the people of London to-night. When
you come to men and extend to them God's wonderful invitation of grace to His royal banquet, one and
and all, instead of accepting it with glad alacrity,
begin to make excuses for not coming. In the
parable from which the text is taken our Lord Jesus
Christ represents that the Gospel invitation is an
invitation to a banquet. So it is. Never was there
such a glorious banquet spread on earth as this
which God spreads for you and me in the Gospel of
His Son, Jesus Christ. God's table is just groaning
with good things. Now, when men are invited to
a royal banquet they begin to cast about for some
way to get to it. But when the great King of
Kings spreads His table and invites His guests, so
great is the blindness and madness of the human
heart that men try to find some excuse for not
going. If at the coronation, a few months ago,
King Edward had given a great banquet in this

city, and sent out invitations to his guests, every
person who was honoured by an invitation would
have moved Heaven and earth to get to that banquet, because they were so honoured that the king
had sent them an invitation. But when the great
King, the Lord God Almighty, sends out His invitation by His Gospel messengers to His royal
banquet, in the desperate wickedness of the human
heart, and in your stubborn rebellion against the
Lord who loves you and gave His Son to die for
you, instead of trying to come to the banquet, you
try to find some excuse for not coming. Our Lord
Jesus Christ, in the parable, gives us three illus-
trative excuses, and each one of these excuses is
perfectly absurd ; and that is the point of it. Our
Lord Jesus wants us to see how utterly irrational
and absurd are all the excuses that men make for
not coming to Christ.

The first excuse was this : " I have bought a
piece of ground, and I must needs go and see it."
How utterly absurd ! It sounds rational at the
first hearing, and looks rational at the first glance,
but when you look at it, how absurd it is. If the
man had already bought the ground, where was the
need of hurry in going to see it ? He could have
waited until the banquet was over. Furthermore,
who ever heard of going out at supper-time, after
dark, to see land ? He was just making up an excuse, and his excuse, like most of yours, was a lie.
If the man had been a real sensible business man
he would have gone and seen the ground before he
bought it. The idea of a man buying a piece of
ground and then going to see it ! I know of a man
in America who did that once. It was up in

Minneapolis. The man bought some real estate in that city, and instead of going to see it first, or sending some one to see it, he had bought it, and months after he thought he would go and see it. He went up there and found his land was at the bottom of Lake Harriet. Very good soil, but too wet!

The second excuse was equally absurd. The man said: " I have bought five yoke of oxen and I go to prove them." How absurd ! There is no hurry ; the oxen were already purchased ; he might go to the banquet first and try the oxen afterwards, and if he had been a real sensible business man he would have tried the oxen first, and bought them afterwards. Anyway, day-time is far better than night-time to try oxen.

The third man's excuse was the most absurd of all. He said, " I have married a wife, and therefore I cannot come." I would like to know why not ? If it had been a funeral there would have been some sense in his excuse, but it was a feast. Who ever saw a bride that was not willing to go to a feast ? Why did he not bring her with him ? There was plenty of room at the feast.

You laugh at those excuses, but I want to ask if there is any one here to-night with a better excuse ? I am going to take up the excuses men bring forward to-day for not coming to Christ, and show you the utter absurdity and unreasonableness of every one of them.

1. The first excuse is this : *there is too much to give up*. That is absolutely unreasonable. You say, " Do you mean to say there is nothing to give up if one comes to Christ ? " No, I say nothing of

the kind. I never knew any one to come to Christ yet that did not have to give up something. The drunkard has to give up his drunkenness, the gambler his gambling; people who are following the frivolities of the world have to give them up. I am not saying there is nothing to give up, but still that excuse is absurd. You say, "Why?" For three reasons. In the first place, the only things God asks you to give up are the things that are doing you harm. We read in Psalm lxxxiv. 11: "The Lord God is a Sun and Shield: the Lord will give grace and glory: no good thing will He withhold from them that walk uprightly." God has given to each one of us a guarantee that He will never ask us to give up anything that is for our good, and that guarantee is His own Son. As we read in Romans viii. 32: "He that spared not His own Son, but delivered Him up for us all, how shall He not with Him also freely give us all things?" I do not think if God has given His Son to die for us, He is going to ask us to give up anything that is good for us. I remember once in an after-meeting, I was talking to a young lady about coming to Christ. She said, "Well, I would like to be a Christian." "Then become one now." "Oh, no," she replied. "Why not?" "There is too much to give up." I said, "See here, do you think God loves you?" "Why, I know He does." "How much do you think God loves you?" "God loved me enough to give His Son to die for me." "Well," I said, "do you think that God, if He loved you enough to give His Son to die for you, will ask you to give up anything that is for your good to keep?" She said, "No, He will not." I said, "Do you want

to keep anything that is not for your highest
good ? " She replied, " No." " Then do you not
think you would better come to Christ right now ? "
She said, " I will," and she did.

The second reason why the excuse is absurd is
this : what you give up is nothing to what you get.
It is very easy to give up tin when you get gold,
and it is very easy to give up sin when you get
God. It is very easy to give up painted glass when
you get diamonds and rubies and emeralds and
pearls instead. And it is very easy to give up the
baubles of the world when you get the real jewels
of Heaven in exchange. I do not think that anybody ever gave up more for Christ than did Paul,
and yet, when he was sore tried and in prison,
writing about what he gave up, he said, " What
things were gain to me those I counted loss for
Christ. Yea, doubtless, and I count all things
but loss for the excellency of the knowledge of
Christ Jesus my Lord, for whom I have suffered the
loss of all things, and do count them but dung, that
I may win Christ." He said, " What I gave up is
nothing to what I gained." You cannot find a
Christian on the face of the earth that will not tell
you that what he gave up for Christ was nothing
to what he got. Suppose there was some young
woman in this town with a pretty face ; a bright
girl, but without very good sense after all, with
a good deal of vanity, and being poor and unable
therefore to buy real jewellery, she bought imitation. She had a brass ring, which she thought
people would think was gold, but no one ever
thought so. Then she had another ring, with two
bits of green glass and a bit of white glass in the

middle, and thought people believed it was a diamond
and emeralds, but they did not. Then she had a
string of white beads round her neck, and thought
people believed they were real pearls, but no one
ever dreamed it. Then she had a pair of earrings
made of brass, with two bits of white glass, and
wished people to believe that they were real diamonds; nobody ever thought of such a thing.
After a while a fine, intelligent, bright, sensible
young fellow falls in love with her. You say that
no sensible fellow would fall in love with a girl like
that. But you cannot tell what a man will do
when he falls in love. One night, after they have
become well acquainted, he says to her, "Mary, I
wish you would throw away that brass ring, and
that ring with the bits of glass in it, and that white
bead necklace, and those pieces of brass and glass
in your ears. To tell you the truth, I am ashamed
about them when I go out with you, and I wish you
would throw them away." She says, "Oh, John, I
think ever so much of you, and would do a good
many things for you, but I cannot do that. They
are the best I have, and I really think people
believe they are genuine." "No, no, Mary, they do
not; they make you a laughing stock, and I wish
you would throw them away." But she says, "Well,
John, I love you, but I really cannot do it." A few
nights after John comes again. He has a big
Russian leather box; he presses a spring, the cover
falls back, and inside it is lined with the very best
of satin, and there is a real gold ring with two
beautiful emeralds and a beautiful diamond, there
is a necklace of real pearls, and there is also a pair
of real diamond earrings. "Look there, Mary;" and

oh, how her eyes sparkle! "Why, John, are they not beautiful! Who are they for?" "Well, Mary, they are for you if you will throw away that brass and glass of yours." How long do you think it would take Mary to throw away her imitation jewels? Oh, men and women, cast all the baubles of this world's pleasures into the fire, and receive the gold and emeralds and rubies and diamonds and pearls of Heaven.

In the third place, the excuse is absurd, because what we give up for Christ is nothing to what Jesus Christ gave up for us. Oh, friends, when we stop to think what Jesus Christ gave up for us, how He left Heaven and its glories and came down to earth and its shame, how He left the songs of praise of angels, and the archangel, and cherubim, and seraphim, and came down here to be despised and rejected of men, to be spat upon and buffeted, to wear a crown of thorns, and to bear the nails in His hands and feet for you and me, how ungrateful, how unreasonable, how base, how black it is for you and me to talk about what we give up for Jesus Christ when we think of what He gave up for us.

2. Another man says, "I have an excuse and a good one. *There are so many hypocrites in the church.*" What shall I say to that excuse? I say without hesitation that that is the most absurd excuse a man can make. "What," you say, "are there no hypocrites in the church?" Of course, there are. The Bible tells us that there will be hypocrites in the church. In the passage which I read to-night Jesus said that there would be hypocrites right up to the judgment day. "Many will say unto Me in that day, 'Lord, Lord, have

we not prophesied in Thy name, and in Thy name have cast out devils, and in Thy name done many wonderful works?' And then will I profess unto them, I never knew you: depart from Me ye that work iniquity."

Of course there are hypocrites in the Church, but I would like to know how that is an excuse for your trampling under foot the Son of God. The fact that another man is a hypocrite is no reason why you should trample under foot the Son of God, God's own Son, Jesus Christ. What would you think of a man here in London refusing his allegiance to King Edward, and saying " No, I will not have him for king; I have got a good reason." " What is it?" " Because there are so many people that profess to be loyal to King Edward who are not." What would you think of that for an excuse? You would think of that man as a fit subject for a lunatic asylum. But that is the way you reason. There are so many people that pretend to be loyal to Jesus who are not, that it excuses you from even professing to be loyal. Bah!

Then again, if there are hypocrites in the Church (and I have no doubt of it), there are a great many good people in the Church. Of course I use the term Church not meaning any one denomination, but the whole body of believers in Jesus Christ. There are a great many good people in the Church; in fact, all the best people are there. But if there were a church or chapel consisting of a hundred members, and ninety-nine were good, straight, upright, downright, Christian men and women, and there was one poor, miserable hypocrite, you would overlook the ninety-nine good straight members, and fix all your attention on the one poor, miserable hypocrite. Yes, you would! And do you know why that is? It is because you are a hypocrite yourself. You are a hypocrite outside the Church, and therefore you are looking for hypocrites inside the Church to hide behind. Did it ever occur to you that you cannot hide behind a thing which is smaller than yourself? You must be a mighty small man or woman to be able to hide behind such a mean hypocrite as that. God will have you out of that hiding-place. Do you know what He says about these men who are always talking about hypocrites in the Church? Turn to Romans xiv. 12: "So then, every one of us shall give account *of himself* to God." You won't have to answer for the hypocrite, but you will have to answer for yourself. A friend of mine was walking in Chicago one night when a young fellow of about thirty walked up, and my friend said to him, " Are you a Christian?" He replied, " No, sir, I am not." " Well, why are you not?" He said, " Because there are so many hypocrites in the Church." My friend said, " I want to show you something," and he opened the Bible at Romans xiv. 12, and said, " Read that." The man read, " and every one of us shall give account of himself to God." My friend said, " Who have you got to give account of?" The man replied, " Of myself." He said, " To whom have you to give account?" The man replied, " To God." He said, " Are you ready to give an account of yourself to God?" and the man sank down on his knees in one of the busiest streets of Chicago, and did what some of you here to-night ought to do; he cried, " God be merciful to me, a sinner."

One more word before I leave this matter. All the hypocrites are going to hell. The Bible says so, and if you keep on rejecting Christ you are going there too. Now I will ask you a question: Which is better, to spend a few years with the hypocrites in the Church here on earth (and with all the good people at the same time), or spend eternity with the hypocrites in hell, with all the bad people? " Well," you say, " that excuse is absurd, and I will never make it again." I hope you never will. You will not if you have any common-sense.

3. But another man says, " I have a good excuse. *I am a pretty good sort of a man;* I do not profess to be perfect, but I think the good in my life will more than balance the evil in my life, and I think God will accept me on the ground of the good I have done and the character I have maintained." What shall I say to that man? I say this to every man and woman in this building to-night who is out of Christ, " You are a very wicked man; you are a very sinful woman. I know you will say, " I am not at all." Yes, you are; and I will prove it to you. I will prove to you that you are so sinful that you have broken the very first and greatest of God's commandments. You may differ from some of your fellow-men and women on the minor moralities, thank God you do. Some men swear, and you do not; some men lie, and you do not; some get drunk, and you do not; some commit adultery, and you do not. On these minor moralities you differ from some of your fellow-men and women, and are better than they. But, on the great question of the treatment of the infinite God, before which all the minor moralities of our treatment of men sink into

utter insignificance, you are all on the same plane,
you have broken the first and greatest of God's commandments. Turn to Matthew xxii. 37 and 38 :
" And Jesus said unto him, Thou shalt love the
Lord thy God with all thy heart, and with all thy
soul, and with all thy mind. This is the first and
great commandment." Have you kept it ? Have
you loved God with all your heart and soul and
mind ? Have you put God first in everything, God
first in business, God first in pleasure, God first in
politics, God first in social life, God first in study,
God first everywhere ? Have you done this ? You
say, " No, I have not." Then you stand convicted
before God of having broken the first and greatest
of God's commandments, of having committed the
very worst sin that a man or woman can commit.
One night after a meeting like this, a friend of
mine, a pastor in Chicago, came to me and said, " I
have a young man who wants to enter the ministry.
I want you to talk to him." He brought up the
young man, and I said to him, " The pastor says
you want to be a minister." He said, " Yes, I
do." I said, " Are you a Christian ? " He answered,
" Why, of course I am. I was brought up as a
Christian, and I am not going back on the training
of my parents." I said, " Have you ever been born
again ? " He said, " What ? " I said, " The Word
of God says ' except a man be born again, he cannot
see the Kingdom of God.' Have you been born
again ? " He replied, " I never heard of that before
in all my life." I said, " Do you know that you
have committed the greatest sin a man can commit ? " He said, " No, I never have." " What do
you think is the greatest sin ? " He said, " Murder,

of course." I said, "You are greatly mistaken. See what the Lord Jesus Christ says about it,"—and I opened the Bible at Matthew xxii. 37, 38, and he read: "Thou shalt love the Lord thy God with all thy heart, and with all thy soul, and with all thy mind. This is the first and great commandment." I said, "Which commandment is that?" He replied, "It is the first and great commandment." I said, "Have you kept it? Have you loved God with all your heart and soul and mind? Have you put God first in everything, God first in business, God first in study, God first in pleasure, God first in everything?" He answered, "No, sir, I have not." "Well, what have you done?" "I have broken this commandment." "Which commandment is it?" "It is the first and great commandment." "What have you done?" He said, "I have committed the greatest sin a man can possibly commit; I have broken the first and greatest of God's commandments, but I never saw it before in all my life."

Probably *you* never saw it before, but you see it to-night. There is no difference. Every man and woman out of Christ has broken the first and greatest of God's commandments, and there is no hope for you outside the atoning blood of Jesus Christ, shed on the Cross of Calvary. When I was in Sydney, I said that at a meeting, and the next day I received a note from a lady, who said, "I wish you would pray for me. I have been trusting in my morality, but you showed me last night that I was a very wicked woman." Oh, may God grant that some of you here to-night, that have been trusting in your goodness, may see that in God's sight you are

Q

very wicked men, very sinful women, for you have broken the first and greatest of God's laws.

4. Another man says, " That excuse is not a good one. I wonder that any intelligent man should ever make it. But I have a good one. *I am too great a sinner to come to Christ.*" Now, I believe people make that excuse honestly. I believe there are a great many people who would like to come, but think they are too bad. What shall I say to them ? What God says in 1 Timothy i. 15 : " This is a faithful saying, and worthy of all acceptation, that Christ Jesus came into the world to save sinners ; of whom I am chief." I remember one Sunday morning in my church, one of the deacons walked down the aisle to a man of about thirty-five years of age, who was standing up. My deacon turned to him and said, " Are you a Christian ? " " No," he said, " I am not." " Why not become one now ? " He replied, " I am too great a sinner to be saved." My deacon said, " Thank God." Then he turned to me and said, " Come here, Brother Torrey. Here is a man who is too great a sinner to be saved, thank God." The man stood there in amazement, wondering what it all meant. But I understood, and I went down and said, " Is that true ? " He said, " Yes, I am too great a sinner to be saved." I said, " Let me show you what God says," and I opened the Bible at 1 Timothy i. 15 : " This is a faithful saying, and worthy of all acceptation, that Christ Jesus came into the world to save sinners, of whom I am chief." " Well," he said, " I am chief." He was a hardened sinner ; he had run away from his wife, and gone up to the North-West ; had gone in for gambling, had laid down 35,000 dollars just a

week before, and was a desperate man. "Well," he
said, "I am chief." I said, "It means you, then."
I said, "Will you accept Jesus Christ right now?"
and he said, "I will," and he dropped down on his
knees and accepted Christ then and there. He
stayed with us about two weeks, went up to the
North-West, and came back again, and every night
was in the meeting leading others to Christ, sent for
his wife, set up a new home, and was so happy that
he adopted a little child out of the orphan asylum
to make his home complete. He was "too great
a sinner to be saved," but he was saved in five
minutes.

5. Another man says, "My excuse is different. *I
cannot hold out.*" Well, that excuse is perfectly
absurd. "Why is my excuse absurd?" Because
God does not ask you to hold out. Holding out
is not your business. That is the business of the
Lord Jesus Christ. We read in Jude, verse 24:
"He is able to keep you from falling and to present
you faultless before the presence of His glory with
exceeding joy." Ah, men and women, there is not
a man who is able to hold out in his own strength.
But, thank God, there is not a man or woman so
weak that Jesus Christ cannot keep him or her. A
man in New York one night was on the verge of
delirium tremens. He had had it again and again.
He had committed 139 forgeries, all against one
man. He went to the Cremorne Mission, and heard
Jerry M'Auley tell how the Lord Jesus Christ had
saved him; and when Jerry said, "If there is any one
wants to be saved to-night, let them come to the
front," he went up the aisle, and said, "Pray for
me." Jerry said, "Pray for yourself," but he did

not know how to pray; he had forgotten how;
the man had gone away down through drink, and
was an outcast. Jerry said, "Pray for yourself."
And Sam Hadley cried out, "God be merciful to
me a sinner," and before he got up he was a transformed man. Some years after I was in Washington, presiding at a conference. Mr. Wanamaker, the
Postmaster-General of the United States of America,
was there, and he said to me, "I want you to come
round to my house to dinner," and I went round.
And when I was ushered into the drawing-room,
who should I see sitting there but Sam Hadley
and his wife, honoured guests in the home of the
Postmaster-General of the United States of America
—the former forger! And there is not a more
honoured man in New York City to-day than Mr.
Samuel Hadley, as he is *now* called.

Oh friends, thank God there is not a man or
woman so weak, so helpless and hopeless, but Jesus
Christ can hold them if they put their trust in Him
to-night.

6. Just one more excuse. Another man says,
"My excuse is a little different. *God won't receive
me if I come.*" People make this excuse in different
ways. "I have sinned away the day of grace, I have
committed the unpardonable sin, and He won't receive me if I come." What shall I say to this? I
will say that excuse is just as absurd as any. Why?
Because it is contradicting God's plain statement in
John vi. 37, "Him that cometh to Me I will in no
wise cast out." Thank God, there is not a man or
woman on the face of the earth, not a man or woman
in London, or in this building to-night, but if you
come to Jesus Christ He will take you and save you.

At one time in Chicago I received a letter something
like this: " I have a son who thinks he has committed the unpardonable sin. He has been for
months in despair, has attempted suicide five times.
I wish you would take him at the Bible Institute."
That was very touching. Nevertheless, I felt it to
be my duty, as the superintendent of the Institute, to
write: " I sympathise with you deeply, but I cannot
take your son. That is not the purpose of the Institute, which is for the training of men and women for
Christian work." He replied, and said, " You must
take him; if you do not, we do not know what to
do." I wrote again that I had the deepest sympathy
with him, but was entrusted with the funds of the
Institute, and it was not right to take his son.
Then some one else wrote to me—a personal friend
—and said, " I want you to take him for my sake."
He had been a great friend of the Institute, and I
now felt that I was warranted in taking the young
man, and wrote telling the father to send him.
They sent him under guard—for they dared not
trust him alone—and he was brought to me. Mr.
Lyon said, " This is Mr. So-and-so. I suppose I can
go now." " Yes," I said, " leave him alone with me."
I said, " Sit down." He looked at me and said, " I
am possessed of the devil." I said, " I guess you
are. But Jesus Christ came to cast out devils."
He said, " I mean that the devil has entered into
me as he did into Judas Iscariot." I said, " That's
very likely, but Jesus Christ is mightier than the
devil, and can set you free from the power of the
devil." He said, " I have committed the unpardonable sin." I said, " Jesus said, ' Him that cometh
unto Me I will in no wise cast out.' " He said, " I

was once enlightened and tasted the gift, I fell away, and it is impossible to renew me again." He knew his Bible, you see! But I said, "Jesus says, 'Him that cometh unto Me I will in no wise cast out.'" He said, "I have sinned wilfully after having received the knowledge of the truth." I said, "But Jesus says, 'Him that cometh unto Me I will in no wise cast out.' Will you come?" Well, he did not come then. Days and weeks passed, and then one day I met him in the Institute, where he was stopping, in the hall-way on the second floor, and I thought the time had come to have it out. I said, "Sit down," and he sat down beside me. I said, "Do you believe the Bible?" "Yes," he said, "I do, everything in it." "Do you believe John vi. 37?" He said, "Yes, and I can quote it: 'Him that cometh to Me I will in no wise cast out.'" I said, "Do you believe that?" "Of course I do; I believe everything in the Bible." "Why do you not come?" He said, "I am possessed with the devil." I said, "The Bible does not say 'Him that is not possessed with the devil if he cometh unto Me I will in no wise cast him out.' It says, 'Him that cometh unto Me I will in no wise cast out.'" He said, "I mean that the devil has entered into me as he did into Judas Iscariot." I said, "It does not say 'Him that the devil has not entered into, if he cometh unto Me, I will in no wise cast out.' It says, 'Him that *cometh* I will in no wise cast out.'" He said, "I have been once enlightened, and have tasted the heavenly gift, and have fallen away, and it is impossible to renew me unto repentance." I said, "It does not say 'If you have not been once enlightened, and tasted the heavenly gift, and fallen away, I will in no wise cast you out.' It says, ' Him that *cometh* unto Me I will in no wise cast out.' " He said, " I have sinned wilfully after I have received the knowledge of the truth." I said, " It does not say ' If you have not sinned wilfully after receiving the knowledge of the truth, if you come unto Me, I will in no wise cast you out.' It says ' Him that *cometh* unto Me I will in no wise cast out.' " He said, " My heart is as hard as the floor." I said, " It does not say ' If your heart is soft and tender, and you come unto Me, I will in no wise cast you out ; ' but ' Him that *cometh* unto Me I will in no wise cast out.' " He said, " I do not feel like coming." I said, " It doesn't say ' If you feel like coming, and come unto Me, I will in no wise cast you out.' It says ' Him that *cometh* unto Me I will in no wise cast out.' " He said, " I don't know that I will come the right way." I said, " It does not say ' If you come the right way I will in no wise cast you out.' It says ' Him that *cometh* unto Me I will in no wise cast out.' " And the young man had got to the end of his rope ! Now, I said, " Will you come ? Get down," and I put my hand on his shoulder and helped him down. I said, " None of your foolishness ; do you believe the Bible ? " He said, " I do." Then I said, " Follow me," and I looked up and said, while he repeated the words after me, sentence by sentence, " O God, I am a miserable sinner, and do not deserve Thy mercy. My heart is as hard as this floor ; I do not feel like coming ; but Jesus says, ' Him that cometh to Me I will in no wise cast out,' and I believe that, just because Jesus says it. Lord Jesus, the best I know, I come." I said, " Did you come ? Did you mean it ? " He said, " I did."

I said, "Follow me again," and he again repeated the words after me, sentence by sentence. "Lord Jesus, Thou hast said, 'Him that cometh to Me I will in no wise cast out.' I have come, therefore Thou hast received me, and I thank Thee." I said, "Has He received you?" He said, "I don't feel it." I said, "I did not ask what you felt; what does Jesus say?" He said, "Him that *cometh* unto Me I will in no wise cast out." "Did you come?" "I did." "What has Jesus done?" "He has received me." "Now," I said, "go right to your room. The devil will give you an awful fight, I have no doubt. But you kneel right down with both knees on John vi. 37, and fight the devil with it, and you believe what God says, no matter what the devil whispers." He went to his room, and the devil gave him an awful time, but he kept both his knees on John vi. 37, and came out with the light of Heaven on his face. He soon began to preach and teach the Bible, and is to-day one of the most useful men on earth.

God's Word is sure, in spite of the devil, in spite of your fear, in spite of everything. And, standing on God's Word, I proclaim to every man and woman in this room that if you come to Jesus Christ He will take you to-night. Will you come?

XVI

HEROES AND COWARDS

"The fear of man bringeth a snare."—PROVERBS xxix. 25.

I HAVE a long text to-night, in fact three texts.
The text is the best part of the sermon. If a
sermon is better than the text it is a poor sermon.
A good sermon is simply an exposition of the text.
You will find the first text in Proverbs xxix. 25 :
" The fear of man bringeth a snare." Whatever
your views about the inspiration of the Bible may
be, you know that this verse is true enough, anyhow.
How many times we have seen that statement of
God's Word fulfilled. How many a man and woman
in London to-night has been snared by the fear of
man, and ruined for time and eternity. For
example, how many a young man has come up
to London, a pure, innocent, upright, temperate
young fellow, and intended to lead a sober, honest,
industrious life in this great city. He knew something about the perils of drink, and was wise enough
not to touch it ; and he comes to London intending
to be what every man and woman ought to be, a
total abstainer. One night this young man goes
out to dinner, and the gentleman at the head of
the table urges him to take a glass of wine. But
this young man refuses ; he says, " I never drink."
The gentleman laughs at him, the other people at

the table chaff him, some say that he is insulting
the host or hostess by not drinking to their health,
and the fear of man brings him into the snare.
He takes his first glass of wine, and that leads on
to another and another and another, and to-night
he is a drunkard on the streets of London, because
of the fear of man, reputation gone, manhood gone,
brain power gone, business capacity gone, everything
gone; the fear of man has proved his temporal and
eternal ruin.   How many a young fellow comes up
to this great city of London, an honest young man,
who has never gambled in his life.   He plays an
occasional friendly game of cards; but one night,
after work, he is out in the company of a few
friends and they are playing cards as usual, and
some one of the group suggests that they should put
up a little stake, only a small amount, just to make
the game interesting.   The young man hesitates,
but they say, "You don't need to gamble, it is only
threepence or sixpence either way; we are not going
to play for high stakes."   He says, "I never gamble;
I believe it is dishonest."   But they laugh at him,
and chaff him, and tell him he should go along to
Sunday School; and he cannot stand their chaff,
and he puts up his first threepenny bit on a game
of cards.   The passion of the gambler, which is a
more consuming passion than that of strong drink
and more ruinous, takes possession of him; he robs
his employer, and to-day he is in prison, because
the fear of man led him to gamble, and ruined him
utterly.

How many a young girl has come up here from
the country, a modest, innocent girl, but without
firm Christian principles.   She lives in very poor

lodgings; and, seeking for a little gaiety and a little brightness in her humdrum life, she goes occasionally to the theatre, goes to dances and gatherings of that sort. She becomes quite infatuated with the dance, and one night a very pleasant and attractive young fellow, with whom she has become acquainted at the dance, makes a subtle suggestion to her that she does not just exactly understand, but at which her modesty revolts, and she repels it with indignation. But he laughs at her. "Why," he says, "you don't understand. I don't mean any harm at all; it is quite a common thing." And that girl has learnt to permit familiarity which no modest girl would allow herself to permit—for the ballroom admits of familiarity which is permitted by decent people nowhere outside of the ballroom. It is the first step to a blasted life, and that girl to-night is an outcast on the streets of London. The fear of man has brought a snare which has ruined her.

My next text is in John xii. 42 and 43 : "Nevertheless among the chief rulers also many believed on Him, but because of the Pharisees they did not confess Him, lest they should be put out of the synagogue. For they loved the praise of men more than the praise of God." Now that was written about Jerusalem in Christ's time, but it sounds just as if it were written about London to-day. How many men there are in London, leading men, just like these chief rulers of Jerusalem, who believe in Jesus Christ in their hearts, but they do not confess Him with their mouths for fear of what men will say of them, for they love the praise of men more than the praise of God. It is moral cowardice. There are hundreds and thousands and tens of thousands of men and women just as fully convinced as I am that Jesus Christ is the Son of God, and yet holding back from open, public confession of Christ because of moral cowardice.

Now turn to the third text, in 2 Corinthians xii. 10. It is a very different picture. In the two texts thus far we have a picture of the moral coward; now we get to the glorious picture of the moral hero: "Therefore I take pleasure in infirmities, in reproaches, in necessities, in persecutions, in distresses, for Christ's sake." Ah, there is a picture worth looking at! A man who was reproached for the name of God, persecuted for his loyalty to the truth, but although they heaped all manner of infamy on him, he looked up with a smiling face and said, "I take pleasure in infamy." Paul went down to Lystra, and because of his loyalty to the truth and his outspoken defence of the truth, they stoned him, after they had almost worshipped him; and they dragged him outside the city. His disciples stood round thinking he was dead. But after a while he rose up again, and went back to Lystra. Then he went to Derbe. Some of the cautious Christian brethren at Derbe, remembering what had occurred at Lystra, doubtless said: "Now, Paul, it is all right to be loyal and to believe on Jesus Christ, but you must be a little more politic. It is no use running so directly against people's prejudices. Now Paul, don't you be quite so out-spoken here, or they will treat you in Derbe just the same as they treated you in Lystra. Now Paul, be a little

more politic, and compromise a little bit." And
that magnificent man looked up and said, "I take
pleasure in infirmities and distresses for Christ's
sake." Men and women, what you need in London
more than anything else is a few men like Paul,
and a few women with the same spirit, men and
women who will stand for Christ and stand for
God's kingdom without compromise, no matter
whom it hurts or what people say. Now my subject to-night, derived from these three texts, is
" Heroes and Cowards."

I wish to say right here at the beginning that
it takes courage to be a Christian, to be a real,
true, outspoken follower of Jesus Christ. You and
I live in a God-hating world; we live in a compro-
mising age—an age in which men professing to be
Christians are trying to please the world and carry
on the Church of Christ so that there will be no
difference between the Church and the world. Now
in a God-hating world like this, and in a compro-
mising age like this, it takes courage to be an
out-and-out soldier of Jesus Christ. It takes more
courage than a great many of you have got. Many
a man to-day who has great courage, who has
courage enough to be a soldier, who has courage
enough to go to war, courage enough to go to the
front, courage enough to stand on the firing line,
and stand in the face of a galling fire from the
enemy's guns, has not courage enough to go back
to the barracks at night and kneel down and say
his prayers, and endure the chaff of his fellow-
soldiers. It takes courage, the sublimest courage,
to be an out-and-out Christian.

But I will give you to-night five reasons why

every man and woman should publicly confess Christ before the world.

1. In the first place, *because He is such a glorious Lord and Master*. There is nothing to be ashamed of in Jesus Christ. A young fellow got up in a meeting (he had been recently converted), and he tried to give a little testimony for Jesus Christ. But he was inexperienced in public testimony and could not talk very well; and, after he had sat down, an old gentleman got up and said, "Young man, you ought to be ashamed of yourself. You cannot preach, and you ought not to try; you ought to be ashamed of yourself." Then the young man rose again and said, "Well, I am ashamed of myself, but I am not ashamed of my Lord." Ah, the trouble with some of you gentlemen is that you are not ashamed of yourselves, though you ought to be, but you are ashamed of the Lord Jesus. I never met an Englishman who was ashamed of Queen Victoria. I would have been ashamed of him if I had met one, she was such a glorious Queen. I have never met an Englishman who was ashamed of King Edward. But glorious a Queen as Queen Victoria was (and though I am an American citizen I believe she was the most glorious Queen that ever reigned on earth), and glorious a King as we expect King Edward to become, the glory of Queen Victoria and the glory of King Edward pales into utter insignificance before the glory of Jesus Christ. Oh, men and women, there is nothing to be ashamed of in Jesus Christ. It is the noblest thing a man can say, "I am a follower of the perfect Man; I am a follower of the Son of God; I am a follower of the One infinitely glorious, Jesus Christ of Nazareth."

2. In the second place, *every man and woman should confess the Lord Jesus publicly before the world for the sake of their influence.* Every man has an influence. There in no man in London that has not an influence. Every one here has an influence, either for Jesus Christ or against Jesus Christ. There is no man or woman or child here to-night who, if they confessed Jesus before the world as their Lord, and lived in accordance with that confession, would not have an influence to bring somebody else to Christ. On the other hand, there is no man, woman, or child here to-night who, if he does not confess Christ, no matter how well he lives, has not an influence against Christ; and the better he lives the more his influence is against Christ, for people look at him and say, " Look at that man; as far as I can see he lives just as well as these professed Christians, and he is not a Christian, does not profess faith in Christ, I don't see the need of becoming a Christian." Oh, every one of you men that are not openly, decidedly, constantly confessing Christ before the world, you have an influence against Jesus Christ.

At one time, when Horace Bushnell was a tutor in Yale College, they had a great revival throughout the college. Horace Bushnell was the most popular tutor in Yale, but he was not a Christian. And the fact that he was not a Christian was a stumbling-block in the way of many of the students. Horace Bushnell knew it, and was greatly disturbed by it. He went home one night in great uneasiness. Something said to him, " You stand right in the way of this work ; if you were a Christian there are dozens of the young men of Yale College that would come

to Christ." " But," said he to himself, " how can I
come to Christ ? I don't believe in the Bible, and
I don't believe that Jesus Christ is the Son of God.
I cannot play the hypocrite, just so as not to stand
in the way of others." He was very uneasy, and
walked up and down his room thinking about it.
Finally, a voice said to him in his heart, " Horace
Bushnell, what do you believe anyhow ? " " Well,
one thing I believe is that there is an absolute
difference between right and wrong." " Well, have
you taken your stand on that which you do believe ?
You talk about what you do not believe, think
about what you do believe. Have you ever taken
your stand on right, to follow it wherever it carries
you, even if it carries you over the Niagara Falls ? "
He said, " No, I never have, but I will." And he
prayed, " O God, if there is any God, show me if
Jesus Christ is Thy Son, and if you will show me
that I will promise to accept Him as my Saviour
and confess Him before the world," and in a short
time the light burst in upon Horace Bushnell's
darkened soul, and he came out on the side of
Christ, and almost every young man in Yale College
was converted.

Oh, friends, if you say you are agnostics, if you
say you are sceptics, have you ever made an honest
attempt to get out of your agnosticism ? If you
have not, your agnosticism is no excuse, none
whatever. Ah, if some of you men and women of
London occupying prominent places and positions,
if you took your stand where you ought to take it
to-night, on the side of truth, scores of others would
come to Christ.

When Mr. Charles G. Finney was preaching at

Rochester, New York, in the thirties, a great many lawyers came to hear him, and one night, away up in the gallery, sat the Chief-Justice of the Court of Appeals of the State of New York. As he sat there listening to Mr. Finney's tremendous logic, the Chief-Justice of the Court of Appeals of New York State became satisfied of the truth of what Mr. Finney preached. Then the question came to him, "Will you come forward like the other ordinary men and women to the "anxious seat?" Something in him said, "It will never do in the world. You occupy the most exalted legal position in New York State; you are the Chief-Justice of the Court of Appeals; it would never do in the world for you to walk down in front, and seek salvation kneeling down at the 'anxious seat.'" He sat there thinking for a while; then he said to himself, "Why not? I am convinced of the truth of that man's position. I know my duty; why should I not do it like any other man?" He got up from his place in the gallery, and went down the stairway, and came up the stairs back of where Mr. Finney was preaching, and Mr. Finney, in the midst of his sermon, felt some one pulling on the skirts of his coat. He turned round, and there stood the Chief-Justice of the Court of Appeals of New York State. He asked, "What is it?" The Chief-Justice replied, "Mr. Finney, if you will call for people to come to the 'anxious seat,' I will come." Mr. Finney stopped his sermon and said, "The Chief-Justice of the Court of Appeals of New York State says if I will call for anxious ones to come to the 'anxious seat,' he will come. I call for anxious ones now"; and the Chief-Justice of the Court of Appeals went

R

down and took his seat in the " anxious seat," and almost every lawyer and barrister in Rochester was converted, and it is said 100,000 people were converted in twelve months in that district.

Ladies and gentlemen, there are some of you here to-night who, if you had the courage of your convictions and came to Christ, not secretly as some of you want to, but walked right out and took your seat down here in front when I called you to do it, it would shake London. Are you men enough to do it? Are you women enough to do it? Your influence may not be as great as that, but all of you have an influence. Will you exert it for Jesus Christ when the time comes to-night?

3. In the third place, *every one should publicly confess Christ before the world, because it is the only way to obtain the fulness of blessing that there is in Jesus Christ.* In Matthew x. 32, 33, are the words of the Master himself: " Whosoever shall confess Me before men, him will I also confess before My Father which is in Heaven ; but whosoever shall deny Me before men, him will I also deny before My Father which is in Heaven." Oh, friends, think of it —to have Jesus Christ confessing you before Jesus Christ the Father in Heaven. A little fellow, a wee little fellow, got up at a meeting one night, with the tears running down his cheeks—he was a little white-haired Swedish boy—and he said, " Friends, if I confess Jesus on earth down here, then will He also confess me up there before the Father," and sat down. That was the best speech that was made that night. Oh, to think of it—to have the Lord Jesus confess your name before the Father in Heaven! In our great Civil War, when one of our generals

won a great victory, it was the custom of the
Member of Congress for his district to propose a
vote of thanks to him on the floor of the American
Congress.   It was the highest ambition of generals
to be thus mentioned upon the floor of Congress.
I remember that grand old hero, General Howard,
once saying to me, " Torrey, there was one proud
day of my life, and that was when a vote of thanks
was moved to me on the floor of Congress by the
whole Congress for my stand at Gettysburg."   But
what is it to be mentioned on the floor of any Parliament or Congress down here to being mentioned
in the court of Heaven by the Lord Jesus Himself ?
And the men and women who confess Christ down
here in Mildmay Hall, Jesus Christ will confess you
before God in Heaven.

Moreover, when Christ does confess you before
the Father, then you will get the fulness of the
blessing.   When He confesses you, then God
sends His Holy Spirit into your heart.   I remember one night in a mission at Atalanta,
Georgia, at the close of the meeting, a young man
of about thirty to thirty-five years of age, was
brought to me.   Some one said to me, " This is one
of the leading advocates of Atalanta.   He took all
the oratorical honours in his university.   I wish
you would lead him to Christ."   I stood a few
moments talking to him, then I said to him, " Are
you not a Christian ? "   He said, " No, sir.   I am a
church member ; in fact, I am the superintendent
of a Sunday School, but I am not a Christian."
"Well," I said, "why don't you become a Christian ? "
He said, " I have no feeling."   I said, " It is not a
question of feeling.   Do you believe you are a

sinner." He said, " I know I am." I said, " Do you
believe Jesus Christ died for you ? " He said, " I
know He did." I said, " Then will you take Him
for your own Saviour to-night ? " He said, " Can I
do it without feeling ? " I said, " Certainly; it is
not a question of feeling, but of common-sense.
Will you take Him ? " He said, " I will; if I can I
will." I said, " Let us pray together." We knelt
and prayed, and when we got up he said, " I don't
feel any different." I said, " I didn't think you
would." " But," he said, " a lot of these people say
they have such joy." I said, " You have not gone
far enough; you have to confess your Lord publicly
before the joy comes." Almost everybody had gone
out of the big Tabernacle ; but he said to the few
who were remaining, " Friends, I have decided to-
night to be a Christian; I have taken the Lord
Jesus Christ to be my Saviour," and with a few
more words he said, " Good-night," and went out.
Next morning a leading merchant of the town came
to me and said, " You ought to have seen what I
saw last night when I left this building. I had
gone only a short way down the street when I saw
—— leaning up against a lamp-post. I knew he
did not drink; I knew he was not intoxicated. I
went up to him and asked him what was the matter,
and why he was shouting. He said, " I am so
happy, I can hardly stand up." I saw him that
day, and I told him what my friend had told me.
I said, " Mr. —— said he saw you leaning against a
lamp-post and shouting, and when he asked you
what was the matter, you said you were so happy
you could not stand up. Is that so ? " He said,
" It was literally true. Ten minutes after I left

you last night, such a joy came over my soul that
literally I had to lean against the lamp-post and
shout for joy."

I don't know if it will affect you just that way;
it never did me; but I will guarantee one thing—
that if you will accept Jesus Christ with all your
heart and surrender your whole life to Him, and His
control, and publicly confess Him before the world,
God will send His Holy Spirit into your heart,
filling it with a joy that you never knew before.

4. In the fourth place, *every man and woman
should confess Christ, because it is the only way
to be saved*. In Romans x. 9 and 10 we read:
" If thou shalt *confess with thy mouth* the Lord
Jesus, and shalt believe in thine heart that God
hath raised Him from the dead, thou shalt be
saved. For with the heart man believeth unto
righteousness; and *with the mouth confession is
made unto salvation*." People say to me in some
places where we go, " I don't believe in this standing up and confessing;" but I don't care what you
believe; the question is, " What does God say?"
And God says, " With the mouth confession is
made unto salvation." There are a great many
people who will tell you if a man or woman believes in Christ in the secrecy of their own hearts
they need never say anything about it, for God
sees the heart. He does see your heart, and if you
do not confess Christ, He sees you have not got any
real faith. You say, " Is not a man saved by faith?"
Yes, but by real faith, and real faith always leads to
mouth confession. We read in the very next verse
of this chapter, Romans x. 11 : " Whosoever be-

lieveth on Him shall not be ashamed." If you are
ashamed to confess Him you do not believe on
Him. A faith that does not lead to confession
will never lead to Heaven. There will be no sneaks
and cowards in Heaven. Jesus Christ says in Mark
viii. 38 : " Whoso shall be ashamed of Me and of
My words, of him also shall the Son of Man be
ashamed, when He cometh in the glory of His
Father with the holy angels."

5. Once more, *every man and woman should confess Christ for common decency's sake and self-respect's
sake.* When you and I stop to think what Christ
has done for us ; how He left Heaven with all its
glory and came down to earth with all its shame ;
how He was scourged and crowned with thorns ;
how He bore shame and reproach ; how He was
spat upon and buffeted and nailed to the Cross
for you and me ; how, although He was rich, yet
for our sakes He became poor, that we through His
poverty might become rich ; how, though being in
the form of God, He thought it not a thing to be
grasped to be equal to God, but humbled Himself
and took upon Himself the form of a servant, and
was obedient even unto death, yea, the death of the
Cross ; how He was wounded for our transgressions,
and bruised for our iniquities—if, men and women,
knowing that, you will not confess Jesus Christ because of the fear of man, or fear of loss in business,
or fear of loss of caste in society, then you are a
coward, a poltroon, an ingrate of the basest and
blackest kind. You cannot get round it ; you know
it is God's truth. I cannot see how any intelligent
man or woman can bear in mind what Jesus has

done for them, and then not confess Him, and still retain their self-respect.

We have some things we are proud of in America, and some things we are ashamed of. One of the things we are proud of in America is this, that all boys and girls in America can get a university education; that the son of the farmer and the day labourer and the washerwoman can get a university education as well as the child of the millionaire. Any boy or girl that is worth educating can go through all degrees of learning in America. Since I have been in Chicago, the grandson of a man who used to work for us at home as our gardener, when I was a boy, has been the mayor of the city of Chicago; and the son of a woman who used to do the cooking in our kitchen has occupied another high position in the city. I rejoice in it; it is one of the things that make me glad to be an American. In North Carolina, one of the poorer States—poor financially, but rich in men—there was a farmer who had a bright boy. He had a poor farm, but he said, "My boy is going to get just as good an opportunity as a millionaire's son;" and that poor farmer worked and scraped until he was able to send that boy to the State university. The boy did well, and his letters home delighted his father's and mother's hearts, and they felt well paid for all their sacrifice. But after awhile the father's heart grew lonely, and he said to his wife, "Mother, I cannot stand it any longer; I just must see the boy." It was a long way from the farm to the university, and he loaded his waggon and started on his long drive, and as he drew near to

the town he said to himself : " Well, won't the boy
be surprised ! He don't know I am coming. Won't
he be delighted to see his old father ? " He whipped
up the old team and hurried on, and entered the
town. He was driving up the hill to the college,
and as he went, whom should he see coming down
but his boy with some gay college companions.
The old man was driving slowly, for it was up hill,
but when he saw the boy he jumped out and rushed
up to him and said, " Oh, my boy, my son ! " The
son was ashamed of his poor old father, and he
straightened himself up and said, " There must be
some mistake, sir ; you are not my father. I don't
know you." I am told—I don't know it to be
positively true—but I am told that father turned
round with a broken heart and went home to die.
I can well believe it. It would break my heart for
my boy to treat me that way.

Men and women, what do you say to a boy like
that ? I say he ought to be horsewhipped. I say
he was an infamous ingrate. But I want to say
that he was not so infamously ungrateful as you
men and women in this hall to-night, who know
that Jesus Christ poured out His life unto death
on the Cross of Calvary, and who are so mean
and contemptible and cowardly that you won't
stand up and confess Him.

I am not going to stop with that story. It is
too dark. I am going to tell you another story—
and thank God it is true—of our home land. A
poor woman in one of our towns, who had to work
for her living, for she was a widow—she took in
washing, I think—had a boy, and he was a bright

boy, and he proved a bright man. I think some of you have heard him. She sent her boy to school. He went through the schools, did well, came out at the very top of his class, and was valedictorian of his class, the highest position, and took a gold medal for special excellence in study. The day he was to graduate he said to his mother: "You know, I graduate to-day, mother." She said, "Yes, I know." "Well, get ready," he said, "it is time to get off to the church"—where the graduating exercises were to be held. "Oh, my boy, I cannot go up there," she said; "I haven't anything fit to wear. Why, all the finest people in the town will be there. You would be ashamed of me if I went." "Ashamed of you, mother?" he said; "never! I owe all I have in the world to you. What is more, mother, I cannot graduate unless you do go; and I won't!" And he helped his mother to get ready, and pinned the old faded shawl round her, and made it look as good as possible, and put on her plain old bonnet, and took her on his arm, and walked down the main street with the plain old mother on his arm to the church. When they got there he took her up the centre aisle, and sat her among the finest people in town. When the time came, he went up to deliver his valedictory address and to receive the gold medal amid the applause of his companions; and when he had received it he walked straight down to where his mother sat, and pinned it on her old faded shawl, and said, "Mother, that belongs to you; you earned it."

That is a boy worth having. Now, ladies and gentlemen, I want to ask a question: Do you mean

to-night to be like that rascally, scoundrelly ingrate,
that was ashamed of his old father and broke his
heart, and be ashamed of that glorious Christ that
died for you ; or will you be like the other boy, and,
knowing that you owe everything to Jesus Christ,
stand up and confess Him to-night, and pin all your
honours where they belong, on Jesus Christ !

XVII

THREE FIRES

"He shall baptize you with the Holy Ghost, and with fire."
—MATTHEW iii. 11.

ONE night, years ago, I was sitting at my desk in
my study late at night, and the work of the day
was done.   There was a great deal of confusion
about my study table, for I had just moved that
day, and had not had time to rearrange my papers.
The work of the day being done, I fell into a
reverie, and as I came out of that reverie I found
myself gently waving back and forth in my right
hand a little four-page leaflet.   I do not know how
it got into my hand.   I suppose I took it off the
table; but I don't even know how it got on to the
table, for I had never seen it before.   I looked at
that leaflet, and I noticed these words across the
top of the leaflet in large print, " Wanted, a Baptism
with Fire."   It immediately fastened my attention.
I said, " That is precisely what I do want; if there is
anybody on this earth that needs fire, it is I," for I
was born, and had grown up cold as an iceberg.
So I read the leaflet.   There was not much in
the leaflet that impressed me, except one text, " He
shall baptize you with the Holy Ghost *and with*

fire ; " and that not only impressed me, it kept ringing in my mind and heart, by day and by night.   I
could not get away from it : " He shall baptize you
with the Holy Ghost *and with fire*."   The following
Saturday evening, when I went to a little gathering
for prayer held at my church, I said to the janitor
of the church, when the prayer meeting was over,
" The promise says, ' He shall baptize you with the
Holy Ghost *and with fire.*' "   A sweet smile passed
over the janitor's face, and there was something about
his look which made me think, " Well, the janitor
seems to know all about it.   I wonder if he has got
something his pastor has not got."   During the
days of the next week, when I sat down in my study,
when I walked the streets, that kept ringing in my
ears : " He shall baptize you with the Holy Ghost *and*
with fire."   Thursday night came, and at the close
of my day's work I knelt down before God, and
asked Him for a text or for a subject for Sunday
evening's sermon.   A brother from London was
going to preach for me in the morning.   The only
text I could see in the whole Bible was, " He shall
baptize you with the Holy Ghost and with fire," and
I said, " Father, I am not to preach on Sunday
morning ; that is a Sunday morning text, and I
don't preach in the morning.   Mr. Inglis is going
to preach then."   I generally preach in the morning
to Christians, and to the unsaved in the evening.
" I want an evening text."   But I could not see
anything, but just that one text, ' He shall baptize you
with the Holy Ghost and with fire."   " Well," I said,
" Father, if that is the text you want me to preach
on, evening or morning, I will preach on it ; but I

want to know." Just then there came looming up
out of the Bible two other texts, and both of these
texts had "fire" in them; and while I was on my
knees God just opened the three texts, and I had
my sermon. The next Sunday night I went to
my church and preached that sermon. When I had
finished it I said, "Now all the friends who want to
be baptized with the Holy Ghost and fire to-night,
and all who want to be saved, come downstairs."
The rooms downstairs were jammed, and when all
who replied to the invitation had found room, I
asked all who wanted to be baptized with the Holy
Ghost and fire to go into the kindergarten room,
and those who wished to be saved to go into
another room, the inquiry room, and the rest to
stay where they were. They began to go into both
rooms; I went into the kindergarten room, where
the people were sitting in the little bits of kindergarten chairs, and so closely packed that I literally
had to step over their heads to get to the platform.
Oh, what a time we had in that room that night!
When I came out I asked my assistant, who was in
charge of the inquiry room, what sort of a time he
had had, and he said, "The Spirit of God was
there; and many people came out into the light."
I asked Professor Towner, the choir-master, who was
left in charge of the third meeting, composed of
those who had not entered either of the two rooms,
and he said, "We had no meeting at all; I could
not say a word; the people got right down on their
knees before God, and talked to Him." I hope
God will bless the Word the same way to-night. I
believe He will.

I. The Baptism with Fire

You will find the first of the three fires in Matthew iii. 11 : " I indeed baptize you with water unto repentance; but He that cometh after me is mightier than I, whose shoes I am not worthy to bear: He shall baptize you with the Holy Ghost and with fire." That is the first of the three fires, the baptism with the Holy Ghost and fire. The baptism with fire—what does it mean? Now we know what it means to be baptized with water—we have seen that—but what does it mean to be baptized with fire ? You will get your answer by asking two things : first, what is fire said to do in the Bible ? and, second, what happened to the Apostles at Pentecost when they were baptized with the Holy Ghost and fire ?

1. The first thing that the Bible says that fire does is, *fire reveals*. In 1 Corinthians iii. 13 we read : " Every man's work shall be made manifest; for the day shall declare it, because it shall be revealed by fire." And the first thing that a baptism with fire does is to reveal what a man really is, to show us to ourselves as God sees us. I remember the night before I preached that sermon, late on Saturday night after the sermon was all arranged, I got down and said, " Heavenly Father, I think I have a sermon for to-morrow night, but I don't believe I have got that of which the sermon speaks. I am going to preach on the baptism with the Holy Ghost and fire, and how can I preach on it if I have not had it ? Now, in order that I may preach an honest sermon, baptize me with fire right now."

God heard the prayer, and the first thing that came to pass was that I had such a revelation of myself as I never had before in all my life. I had never dreamed that there was so much pride, so much vanity, so much personal ambition, so much downright meanness in my heart and life as I saw that night. And men and women, if you get a baptism with fire, I believe one of the first things that comes to you will be a revelation of yourself as God sees you. Is not that just what we need, a revelation of ourselves to-day that will spare us the awful humiliation of the revelation of self in that day when we stand before the judgment seat of Christ?

2. The second thing that fire does is, *fire refines*, or purifies. In Malachi iii. 1–3, we are told of the purifying power of fire. There is nothing that purifies like fire. Water will not cleanse as fire does. Suppose I have a piece of gold, and there is some filth on the outside of it; how can I get it off? I can wash it off with water. But suppose the filth is inside it, how will you get it out? There is only one way: throw it into the fire. And, men and women, if the filth is on the outside it can be washed away with the water of the Word; but the trouble is that the filth is on the inside, and what we need is the fire of the Holy Ghost penetrating into the innermost depths of our being, burning, burning, burning, cleansing. What a refining came to the apostles on the day of Pentecost! How full of self-seeking they had been up to the very last Supper! At the Last Supper, they had a dispute as to who should be the first in the Kingdom of Heaven, but after Pentecost they no longer thought of self

but of Christ. How weak and cowardly they had
been right up to the crucifixion! They all forsook
Him and fled, and Peter denied Him, at the accusation of a servant maid, with oaths and curses. But
after the day of Pentecost, that same Peter that
cursed and swore and denied Christ when the servant maid accused him of being a follower of Jesus,
faced the very council that condemned Him, and
said, " If we this day be examined of the good deed
done to the impotent man, by what means he is
made whole, be it known unto you all, and to all
the people of Israel, that by the name of Jesus
Christ of Nazareth, whom ye crucified, whom God
raised from the dead, even by Him doth this man
stand here before you whole." Ah, friends, cleansing
is a very slow process by ordinary methods, but a
baptism with fire does marvels in a moment.

3. In the third place, the Bible teaches us that
fire consumes. In Ezekiel xxiv. 11–13, we are told
of the consuming power of fire, the fire of judgment
that will consume the filth and dross of Jerusalem.
And the baptism of fire consumes, in fact it cleanses
by consuming; it burns up all dross, all vanity, all
self-righteousness, all personal ambition, all ungovernable temper.

We had once at the Bible Institute in Chicago a
young woman who was much that a Christian
should not be. When we heard she was coming,
all of us in authority thought she never ought to
have come to the Bible Institute. I thought so
when I heard she was coming, for I had known her
in the school from which she came, and I knew she
was one of the most unmanageable scholars they

ever had in the school. She was stubborn, wilful,
proud, quick-tempered, boisterous, loud, and pretty
much everything a girl ought not to be. When I
heard she was coming to the Bible Institute, I said,
" So-and-so coming to the Bible Institute! What
in the world does she want at the Bible Institute ? "
But her uncle was one of the best friends the Institute ever had, and so, out of consideration for her
uncle, we admitted her. Now, we require of every
student in that Bible Institute that some definite
work to save the lost should go hand in hand with
Bible study; for Bible study, unless it is accom-
panied with actual work for the salvation of souls,
will dry up a man's soul quicker than almost anything else. We required the young woman to go
into the tenements, the homes of the poor and the
outcast. One afternoon this girl had been visiting
in Milton Avenue and Townsend Street, two of the
poorest streets of Chicago. After a time she became
very tired with climbing up and down the stairs,
and going in and out of the filthy homes; and
instead of returning to the Institute, she walked on
in a very rebellious frame of mind, and went down
to the Lake Shore Drive, the finest avenue in Chicago,
along the shore of the lake. As she passed by those
magnificent mansions there, she looked up at them
with an eye that danced with pleasure, and said,
" This is what I like. I have had enough of Milton
Avenue; I have had enough of climbing stairs and
going into tenements. This is what I like, and this
is what I am going to have." She came back to the
Institute, and went straight to her room, still in a
very bitter and rebellious frame of mind. The tea-

s

bell rang before the battle was over, and she went to the table and took her place, and sat down, and there at the tea-table the fire of God fell right where that girl was sitting. She sprang from her seat and rushed over to a friend at another table, and threw her arms around her, and exclaimed, " I am a volunteer for Africa ! " and the fire of God in a moment burned, and burned, and burned, until that young woman was so changed, her actions were so changed, her views of life; her tastes, her ambitions, her very face was so changed in a moment, that when her old friends saw her and heard her they could hardly believe their own eyes and ears. Later on she went back to that same school down in Massachusetts, where she had been such a hindrance, and with burning words poured out her heart to the girls there, and with mighty power led them to the Lamb of God which taketh away the sins of the world.

Is not that what we need to-night, a fire that will burn up this pride of ours, this selfishness of ours, this vanity of ours, this worldliness of ours, burn up all these things that hinder the world from coming to Christ, because we make men think that Christianity is unreal ? You women with unconverted husbands, is not that what you need, a baptism with fire, transforming your life and clothing it with beauty, so that your husbands will say, " I must have what my wife has got ? "

4. In the next place, *fire illuminates.* Oftentimes when in Chicago I look off towards the north-west of the city, suddenly I see the heavens lit up and then grow dark again, then they are illuminated once more, and then darkened. The great foundry doors

had been opened and shut, and opened and shut, and this light in the heavens was the glow from the furnaces. Fire illuminates, but no fire illuminates like " the baptism with the Holy Ghost and fire." When a man is baptized with the Holy Ghost and fire, truth that was dark to him before becomes instantly as bright as day; passages in the Bible that he could not understand before become as simple as A B C, and every page of God's Holy Word glows with heavenly light. A baptism with fire will do more to take the infidelity and scepticism and false doctrine out of a man than any university education. How many a young fellow comes out of a theological education more than half an infidel, but the great day comes when that half-infidel preacher is baptized with the Holy Ghost and fire, and his doubts and his questionings and his criticisms go to the winds. How many an untaught or half-taught man has so wonderful an acquaintance with the truth of God that men who are scholars sit at his feet with profound astonishment, because he has been illuminated with the baptism with the Holy Ghost and fire !

Take the case of this girl again. I was away when the event I described happened, and the first thing I heard when I returned was what had taken place with her. I was going from the men's side of the institute, and was passing between the church and the women's department when this young girl turned into the gate and met me. She looked up into my face, and said, " Oh, Professor Torrey, have you heard ? " " Yes, Jack, I have heard," I said, and, by the way, that is an indication of her character

that she should be called Jack; "I have heard
what has happened," and then she just began to pour
out her soul. She fairly danced on the side-walk
as she told me, and I knew for once what it meant
to dance before the Lord! Then she closed about
this way: "One of the best things about it is that
the Bible is a new book. The Bible used to be just
the stupidest book I ever read, and I didn't believe
it was the Word of God at all. I did believe in the
divinity of Jesus Christ, because your lectures compelled me. But the Bible was a stupid book. But
oh, now God is showing me such wonderful things
in the Bible."

Now be honest. Are there not some of you
to-night that profess to be Christians, to whom the
Bible is a stupid book? If you would tell the
honest truth, would you not rather read a novel
than the Bible? You do read the Bible, because
you think you ought to; but you get no enjoyment
out of it. What you need is a baptism with the
Holy Ghost and fire, and that would make the Bible
a new book; glory would shine from every page.

5. The next thing that fire does is, *fire makes
warm, it makes to glow.* You stand before a furnace
door, behind which is a glowing fire. You have in
your hand a bar of iron; it is cold, and black, and
forbidding, and there is no beauty in it. But you
take that cold, dark, forbidding bar of iron, and you
open the furnace door and thrust it into the glowing
fire. Soon it is warm, then it becomes red hot and
glows with marvellous beauty, and you have the
cold bar of iron glowing with fire. You and I are
cold—oh, how cold we are! and the Lord Jesus

takes us and He plunges us into the fire of the Holy
Spirit. We begin to grow warm, and soon we glow,
glow with love to God, glow with love to Christ,
glow with love to the truth, glow with love for
perishing souls. Men and women, the great need
of the day is men and women on fire. Brethren,
that is what we need in the pulpit, ministers on fire.
What cold men most of us preachers are! Orthodox
enough, it may be, and we present the most solemn
truth with great force of reason and great beauty
of rhetoric and most convincing eloquence; and
our audiences sit there and admire our strong
preaching, but they do not repent of their sins.
Why not? Because we are not on fire. We con-
vince the intellect, but we do not melt the heart.
But put a minister who is on fire in the pulpit.
Wesley was such a man; Whitefield was such a
man; Charles G. Finney was such a man—put
a man on fire in the pulpit, and the audience
will melt. But we need that kind of people in
the choir as well. What beautiful choirs we have
nowadays. Why, they sing almost like angels,
and people sit there admiring them, but nobody
is converted by their singing. But when we get
a man on fire to sing, or a woman on fire to sing,
or a choir on fire to sing, something is brought
to pass. That is what we need in our Sunday
School classes. We set a young man or a young
woman to teach a Sunday School class, and they
know the lesson capitally and study all the latest
" helps," and make the lesson tremendously interesting, but the boys and girls and men and women in
their classes are not converted, because the teachers

are not on fire.   Oh, men and women of London, the
need in London more than anything else to-night is a
baptism with fire on the minister, a baptism with fire
on the elders, a baptism with fire on the deacons, a
baptism with fire on the choir, a baptism with fire on
the Sunday School teachers, a baptism with fire on the
personal workers, and a baptism with fire upon the
men and women in the congregation.   We sang a
hymn just now, praying that the fire of God might
fall in Mildmay Conference Hall to-night.   If it
does, men and women, if it does, London will be
shaken.

6. The next thing that fire does is, *fire imparts
energy*.   The men of science tell us that every form
of energy can be transmuted into fire, and that given
fire you can generate any form of force or energy.
When a baptism with fire comes then comes power.
That was the principal manifestation at Pentecost.
The fire of God fell, and with the energy of that fire
men went out from that upper room, and 3000
people were converted.   A man takes me to his
factory.   He says, " This machinery is the best in
the world."   He takes me down into the engine-room,
and says, " Look at that great engine, it is so many
horse-power, and there is power in that engine to
move every wheel in this great factory."   Then I go
back to the factory, and I look around.   There is
nothing doing at all.   " It is very strange," I say ;
' did you not tell me that this was the best machinery
in the world for this purpose ? and that that engine
downstairs could move every wheel in the factory ?
Well, I notice the connections are all made, and
everything is in gear, and the lever is carried the

right way, but there is not a wheel moving in all
the factory. What is the matter?" "Don't you
know?" he says. "Come downstairs, and I will
show you," and he takes me down again to the
engine-room to the engine, and he throws open the
door and says, "Look in there." And lo! there is
no fire in the fire-box. I go off to the railway.
There is a great engine standing on the rails, and I
am told it is the finest engine that was ever turned
out from the locomotive works. It can drag a
heavily freighted train up a hundred-foot grade. The
engine has been coupled on to about half-a-dozen
unloaded cars. I look at the engine and say, "What
did you tell me? Can it draw a heavily loaded
train up a hundred-foot grade? Then will you
please explain something to me? That engine has
only six empty cars behind it, the coupling is made,
the throttle is open, and yet it is not moving, and
cannot pull a car, and yet you say it can pull a
hundred. What is the matter?" I am taken on
to the engine, and the door of the furnace is thrown
open, and when I look in I see there is no fire in
the fire-box. That is what is the matter.

Friends, I go into churches to-day, and oh, what
beautiful organisation I see, what magnificent archi-
tecture, what eloquent preaching I hear, what marvellous singing! And yet not a wheel in the whole
institution moving for God. What is the matter?
There is no fire in the fire-box. What we need to-
day is the fire of God in the fire-box, and thank
God the promise is "He shall baptize you with the
Holy Ghost and fire."

7. One thing more about this fire—*fire spreads;*

nothing spreads like fire. I remember hearing some years ago, before I went to live in Chicago, about an old Irish woman, who had a little shanty in the city, with a little shed back of it, in which she kept a cow. And one night she was milking her cow, and the cow suddenly kicked and knocked over her lantern. The lantern fell on a wisp of straw, which caught fire, and set the shed afire. The shed set the shanty afire, and the shanty next to it caught fire, and the shanty next to that, and the one next to that, and soon the fire leaped over the south branch of the Chicago river to the east side, and on and on it swept, and in forty-eight hours it had cleared an area of one mile wide and three miles long, and there were but two buildings left in all that section of Chicago. Fire spreads. If a fire is kindled here to-night it will sweep all over London, and all over Great Britain, and Ireland.

That night I spoke of at the beginning of my sermon, we had a stranger from London in Chicago, who came to hear me preach. He came downstairs in response to my invitation, and he told us, "I am just in Chicago to-day from London, and I want this baptism of fire;" and he got it. When he left the church he went to his room, and sat down and wrote a letter to the Bible class of which he was a member in London. The teacher read it to the class, and the fire of God came into that class, and in about two weeks after he had sent the letter he got word from London that the fire which fell in Chicago had been kindled in that church in London. Nothing spreads like fire. Do we not need the baptism with this fire to-night?

II. THE FIRE OF JUDGMENT THAT WILL TRY
THE BELIEVER'S WORKS

The second fire you will find in 1 Corinthians iii.
13, 15 : " Every man's work shall be made manifest :
for the day shall declare it, because it shall be revealed
by fire ; and the fire shall try every man's work of
what sort it is.   If any man's work shall be burned,
he shall suffer loss : but he himself shall be saved ;
yet so as by fire." This second fire is the fire
of judgment, testing our works at the judgment
seat of Christ.   Now you notice the judgment here
is not the judgment regarding our salvation.   These
are saved people whose works are burnt up.   All the
work we do for Christ is to be put to the test, is to be
put to the severest kind of test, the fire test ; and
friends, there is a great deal the Church of Christ is
doing professedly for Christ, and a great deal that
individual Christians are doing, that will never
stand the fire test.   Do you think that these church
fairs and bazaars and all that sort of tomfoolery by
which the Church of Christ is brought down to the
level of the dime museum, into which so many professed Christians are putting their best energies, do
you think that these will stand the fire test ?
Never ! they will all go up in smoke.   You may be
saved, but you will lose your reward.   You will be
saved so as by fire.   A great deal of work that is
good, but that is done not to God's glory but for
personal ambition — the good sermon, perfectly
orthodox, severely logical, beautifully rhetorical, the
sermon that even good people applaud, but that is
preached not that God may be glorified in the sal-

vation of sinners, but that the preacher may be applauded. Do you think that will stand the fire test? Never! it will go up in smoke. The beautiful solos sung, the philanthropic work done, the personal soul-saving work done, not for God's glory but for the exaltation of self—will these stand the fire test? Never! they will all go up in smoke.

On the night of which I have been speaking in my church, the two leading singers went down into that second meeting, and the leading soprano said—a beautiful singer, one of the most beautiful singers I have ever heard, "I never thought of it before. I don't believe I have sung a solo in my life for God. I sang it for self." Thank God the fire of God came upon my leading soprano and my leading contralto, and I lost them both, for they became missionaries. I would like to lose the whole choir, if I could lose them the same way!

Furthermore, let me say, good work, work done for a good purpose, but done in our own strength and not done in the power of the Holy Ghost, will not stand the fire test. The sermon preached to glorify God, but preached with the enticing words of man's wisdom and not in demonstration of the spirit and power of God, will it stand the fire test? Never! So, men and women, our work is to be tried regarding its character, regarding its motive, regarding the power in which it is done. Will your work stand the fire?

III. The Fire of Eternal Doom

We come now to the third fire. We read of it in 2 Thessalonians i. 7–9: "The Lord Jesus shall be

revealed from Heaven with His mighty angels, in
flaming fire, taking vengeance on them that know
not God, and that obey not the Gospel of our Lord
Jesus Christ. Who shall be punished with everlasting destruction from the presence of the Lord,
and from the glory of His power." The third fire is
the fire of eternal doom. Every one of us must meet
God in fire somewhere. Some of us, I hope, to-night
will meet Him in the fire of a baptism with the Holy
Ghost and fire; some of us, I know, will meet Him
in that great judgment day, when the fire will try
our work, of what sort it is; and oh, friends, some of
us, I fear—God grant it may be very few—may meet
Him in the fire of eternal doom. Some one says,
"Do you think it is literal fire?" I will not stop
to discuss that. Take it as a figure if you will, but
remember that figures always stand for facts. Some
people, if they find anything in the Bible that they
do not like, say "It is figurative," and they think
that has swept it all away. Remember who uses
the figures; they are God's figures; and God's figures
stand for facts, and God is not a liar, so God's figures
never overstate the facts they represent. And how
terrible must be the mental and spiritual agony described by that figure, if figure it be. Were you ever
severely burnt? Did you ever see any one severely
burnt? I have been. And how awful must be the
spiritual or physical agony, whichever it is, that is
represented by such a terrific figure as this.

The superficial thinker says, " Oh, I cannot believe
that; I cannot believe that a merciful God is going
to let men go on suffering day after day, week after
week, month after month, and year after year, with

no hope." Open your eyes. Look at what is going on right around you in London. Is not God permitting men and women who sin, especially in certain specific forms of sin, to suffer most awful agonies day after day, month after month, year after year, without one hope of relief unless they repent; and when the time of possible repentance is passed—and it must pass some time—when the time of possible repentance is passed, and this goes on and on and on, ever worse and worse, what have you got but hell? You don't get rid of hell by getting rid of the Bible, or by getting rid of God; hell is here; hell is a fact in London to-night. The only change the Bible and God make is that they open a door of hope, and when you banish God and the Bible the only change you make is that you shut the only door of hope. The infidels are guilty of the amazing folly of trying to close hell by shutting the only door of hope. Hell is here. It is a present-day fact, and unless there is repentance and acceptance of Christ it will be an eternal and endless fact. You say, "For whom?" Listen: "Rendering vengeance to them that know not God, and to them that obey not the Gospel."

First, "to them that know not God." That is plain English for agnostics. Do you know what "agnostic" means? A great many people are proud of saying, "I am an agnostic." Well, agnostic means "know not" or "know nothing"; it is used of those who "know not God." So our text says God will render vengeance to agnostics. Some one says, "That is not just." I cannot help that; it is a fact. But it *is* just. You *ought* to know God; you have no excuse for not knowing God. The most solemn duty that lies upon every man is to find out about God, and there is a way to know God. The trouble is you don't want to know God. Any agnostic that wants to know God will soon get acquainted with Him. I was once an agnostic, but I was an honest one, and I did not take long to find God.

Only the other night a man said to me, " I am an agnostic." I pointed him to a way out of agnosticism, a reasonable way, and asked, "Is not that reasonable?" and he said " Yes." Then I said, " Will you try it ? " and he said " No, I won't." His agnosticism is not his misfortune; it is his sin. The first and most solemn obligation resting on the creature is to know and worship and serve the Creator. You ought to know God, and if you refuse to know Him, the Lord Jesus will be revealed at last rendering vengeance to you and other agnostics.

But not only to agnostics, but " to them that obey not the Gospel." Many a man is not an agnostic, but he does not obey the Gospel. There are many of you people who would support what I say about agnosticism, but you do not obey the Gospel. You do not believe with real faith, which means absolute surrender to and confidence in the Lord Jesus Christ. You do not obey Jesus Christ as your Lord and Master. You do not openly confess Him as the Gospel commands. He will render vengeance to you; you shall be " punished with everlasting destruction from the presence of the Lord and from the glory of His power."

Men and women, every one of us must meet God in fire. Oh, to-night do you not want to meet Him in the glorious fire of the Holy Ghost, refining you from sin, cleansing the dross and filth, illuminating you with God's glorious truth, warming the cold heart until it glows with holy love, energising you with the power of God, and spreading wherever it goes? Or do you wish to meet God in fire at that judgment day, that will try your work as to character, motive, the power that wrought it, and send all your works up in smoke, and leave you there stripped, saved "so as by fire?" Or will you meet God in that awful fire of eternal doom, when the day comes that the same Christ whom you have rejected and trampled under foot comes back again in the glory of the Father, with His mighty angels, "rendering vengeance to them that know not God and obey not the Gospel?"

THE END